Article 17

Access to a Diversity of Mass Media Sources

A Commentary on the United Nations Convention
on the Rights of the Child

Editors

André Alen, Johan Vande Lanotte, Eugeen Verhellen,
Fiona Ang, Eva Berghmans, Mieke Verheyde, and Bruce Abramson

Article 17

Access to a Diversity
of Mass Media Sources

By

Sherry Wheatley Sacino

LEIDEN • BOSTON
2012

Cover image by Nadia, 1½ years old.

This book is printed on acid-free paper.

Library of Congress Cataloging-in-Publication Data

Sacino, Sherry Wheatley.
   Article 17 : access to a diversity of mass media sources / by Sherry Wheatley Sacino.
      p. cm. — (Commentary on the United Nations Convention on the Rights of the Child,
ISSN 1574-8626)
   Includes bibliographical references.
   ISBN 978-90-04-14918-2 (pbk. : alk. paper) 1. Freedom of information. 2. Convention on
the Rights of the Child (1989). Article 17. 3. Mass media—Law and legislation. 4. Children
(International law) 5. Children's rights. I. Convention on the Rights of the Child (1989).
Article 17. II. Title.
   K3255.S23 2012
   341.4'8572—dc23

                                                                                      2011040788

ISSN 1574-8626
ISBN 978 90 04 14918 2 (hardback)
ISBN 978 90 04 21692 1 (e-book)

PRINTED BY DRUKKERIJ WILCO B.V. - AMERSFOORT, THE NETHERLANDS

CONTENTS

LIST OF ABBREVIATIONS

ACLU	American Civil Liberties Union
ACHPR	African Charter of Human and Peoples' Rights (adopted 1981, entered into force in 1986)
African Children's Charter	African Charter on the Rights and Welfare of the Child (1990)
CRC	Convention on the Rights of the Child (1989)
CRC Committee	Committee on the Rights of the Child
CSPA	Columbia Scholastic Press Association
IFJ	International Federation of Journalists
MAP	Media Access Project
NGO	Non-governmental Organization
NSPA	National Scholastic Press Association
SPLC	Student Press Law Center
UDHR	Universal Declaration of Human Rights (1948)
UNESCO	United Nations Educational, Scientific and Cultural Organization
UNICEF	United Nations Children's Fund
UNRWA	United Nations Relief and Works Agency
VCLT	Vienna Convention on the Law of Treaties
WAN	World Association of Newspapers

AUTHOR BIOGRAPHY

Sherry Sacino is a lifelong journalist and entrepreneur having founded and operated two news services *Athletes News Service* and *Youth OUTLOUD!* for a combined total of twenty years. She currently is the President and CEO of Youth Empowerment Alliance, Inc. and Editor-in-Chief of *Youth OUTLOUD!*, a worldwide distribution network of youth-created media. She holds an Master of Advanced Studies in Children's Rights from the Law Faculty of University of Fribourg/Institut Universitaire Kurt Bösch (IUKB) (Switzerland), and a Bachelor of Arts degree in Journalism from Arizona State University. She lives in St. Petersburg, Florida, New York City and San Sano, Italy.

ACKNOWLEDGEMENTS

This commentary would not have been completed without the unbridled support and human rights legal expertise of Bruce Abramson. The legal interpretation, and scope of Article 17 was written by Bruce, and his tireless efforts are deeply appreciated. In addition, the staff of Stetson University Law Library (especially Pamela Burdett) and staff of The Poynter Institute for Media Studies (especially David Shedden and Karen Brown Dunlap)—all located in St. Petersburg, Florida (USA) were very generous with their resources and commitment to this Commentary. And special thanks to Kelley Benham French for her proofreading and honest comments.

And, thanks to my loyal friends who learned more about Article 17 than they wanted during the past 18 months, and special thanks to my devoted husband, Ron.

FOREWORD

Jean Zermatten[1]

Human Rights have evolved during the past century.

In 1989, a distinct category of rights emerged and remains an underestimated revolution, to recognize the child as a full person—consequently an autonomous rights' holder—who can make decisions and take action according to their own level of maturity. This new concept in international law for children not only provides for the traditional protection (idea of vulnerability) and for services (idea of dependency), but also includes provisions, which empower children, who are seen as individuals with an evolving capacity.

This new status of rights holder is expressed principally by the recognition of two general principles of the Convention on the Rights of the Child:

- the best interests of the child (Art. 3)
- the right of the child to be heard (Art. 12).

These two provisions are complementary, "...one establishes the objective of achieving the best interests of the child and the other provides the methodology for reaching the goal of hearing either the child or the children."[2]

Furthermore, the CRC contains provisions which explicitly grant children civil rights and freedoms, by repeating (partly) provisions of the International Covenant on Civil and Political Rights (ICCPR) and adjusting them to the particular situation of children.[3] In the CRC's initial proposal, such rights as "freedom of expression," "association," "peaceful assembly," "freedom of thought, conscience and religion," and "access to information" were not mentioned. It also did not provide for the right of the child to respect for her/his privacy, family, home and correspondence. It is in the legislative phase that these rights were discussed and proposed and then adopted as integral part of the treaty.

The challenge of considering a child as a person who can exercise rights requires a significant change in the society's state of mind and considerable efforts to fully

---

[1] Director of the International Institute for Children's Rights (IDE), Sion, Switzerland, Chairperson of the UN Committee for the CRC.
[2] GENERAL COMMENT No. 12 (2009), The right of the child to be heard, par. 74.
[3] See Art. 12–17 CRC.

embrace this new paradigm. Respect for civil rights and freedoms is not linked to the economical situation of a State, but rather to its acceptance of its changing attitudes toward children. Creating new laws is not difficult; the problem is to change societal norms; and the State is the expression of the adults' collective will and perceptions.

As a result of the CRC's provisions on the civil rights and freedoms of the child, international law in this area has been improved. Some activities of children, such as peaceful assembly and association, are now specifically guaranteed to children, providing a strong legal basis in international law and many national laws.

For others, including for the right to information (Art. 17), new problems have emerged. The free flow of information, its diversity of sources, the access to information and development of mass media technologies have changed dramatically, and pose new problems for adults and governments especially those in the balance between protection and empowerment of children. Understanding that in 1989, the internet widely unknown, and it would have been impossible to predict its proliferation, especially among the *youngest* people. We are now faced with a delicate and complex question: how to consider the CRC's Article 17 in this totally new, constantly evolving context, where the children are the teachers and their parents the pupils?

When we evoke the new technologies, the main concern of adults is not to mention the benefits of them, but rather to denounce the dangers of the new phenomenon as it applies to children, specifically:

- Sexually explicit or provocative materials
- Program Violence
- Violation of privacy
- False or Misleading information

This underscores the necessity of parents and government to oversee and educate, for the creators of information to respect code of ethics and for children themselves to be able to interpret and dissect information, as to develop a critical attitude and self-governance.

How does the international community bring together this creativity, novelties and technical achievements with the idea of rights, the necessity of control and protection while fulfilling the obligations of the governments?

It's the challenge of this Commentary written by Sherry Sacino. I'm very proud to welcome this scientific contribution of one of the former participants in Master of Advanced Studies in Children's Rights;[4] and I'm very grateful to Sherry to have taken up this difficult task and to have approached the question not only from the point of view of the legal analysis of Article 17 (with expert Bruce Abramson's collaboration), but especially to have handled the problems of the implementation of the many aspects of the article, in the various contexts and settings.

I'm sure this Commentary will help all the actors of both human rights and children rights—including the professionals working within information development and dissemination—in this broader interpretation of the CRC's Article 17, as understood via this contemporary approach.

---

[4] Master of Advanced Studies in Children's Rights (MCR), IUKB University, Sion, Switzerland http://www.iukb.ch/uer-droits-de-lenfant/enseignements/master-of-advanced-studies-in-childrens-rights-mcr.html.

TEXT OF ARTICLE 17

ARTICLE 17

States Parties recognize the important function performed by the mass media and shall ensure that the child has access to information and material from a diversity of national and international sources, especially those aimed at the promotion of his or her social, spiritual and moral well-being and physical and mental health. To this end, States Parties shall:

(a) Encourage the mass media to disseminate information and material of social and cultural benefit to the child and in accordance with the spirit of Article 29;

(b) Encourage international co-operation in the production, exchange and dissemination of such information and material from a diversity of cultural, national and international sources;

(c) Encourage the production and dissemination of children's books;

(d) Encourage the mass media to have particular regard to the linguistic needs of the child who belongs to a minority group or who is indigenous;

ARTICLE 17

Les Etats parties reconnaissent l'importance de la fonction remplie par les médias et veillent à ce que l'enfant ait accès à une information et à des matériels provenant de sources nationales et internationales diverses, notamment ceux qui visent à promouvoir son bien-être social, spirituel et moral ainsi que sa santé physique et mentale. A cette fin, les Etats parties:

(a) Encouragent les médias à diffuser une information et des matériels qui présentent une utilité sociale et culturelle pour l'enfant et répondent à l'esprit de l'article 29;

(b) Encouragent la coopération internationale en vue de produire, d'échanger et de diffuser une information et des matériels de ce type provenant de différentes sources culturelles, nationales et internationales;

(c) Encouragent la production et la diffusion de livres pour enfants;

(d) Encouragent les médias à tenir particulièrement compte des besoins linguistiques des enfants autochtones ou appartenant à un groupe minoritaire;

(e) Encourage the development of appropriate guidelines for the protection of the child from information and material injurious to his or her well-being, bearing in mind the provisions of Articles 13 and 18.	*(e) Favorisent l'élaboration de principes directeurs appropriés destinés à protéger l'enfant contre l'information et les matériels qui nuisent á son bien-être, compte tenu des dispositions des articles 13 et 18.*

CHAPTER ONE

INTRODUCTION

Writing the Commentary for Article 17 has proven to be a moving target—one with an undefined role of the mass media interwoven with present-day movement of the role of the mass media and a concrete legal basis. Diligent research and meticulous examination brought to light an interpretation of Article 17 that provides a striking contrast to the assumption of what so many others had once believed it to be, and as it has been previously defined. Article 17 could potentially become one of the most significant legal mechanisms in shaping the flow of information and communication today.

To provide adequate commentary on Article 17, it was essential to thoroughly examine the wording of the text independently as well as in collaboration and comparison with the other articles.

The duty of Article 17 is much more narrow than commonly understood, yet the mass media is more far-reaching than it once was. While the CRC combines all mass media into one category, it is not one industry, but a diverse collection of industries with multiple State and non-state actors, all operating with varying rules of self-governance and legal contexts. A musician does not create lyrics bound by a set of ethical guidelines as the professional journalist has pledged to uphold. Yet, the journalist's role in society has become blurred with the prolific use of the Internet by the 'citizen journalist' and new media storytellers who are void of their societal responsibilities to verify facts, report the truth and present multiple viewpoints in a story.

The flow of information and the development of mass media technologies have dramatically changed since the drafting of the CRC by the Working Group in 1980. Yet, these rapid changes could potentially elevate Article 17 to the primary equalizer in the child's access to a wide variety of information.

Mass media, during the drafting of the CRC, was generally interpreted to mean information that was printed or broadcast to the masses, usually via radio, television, magazines or newspapers. This information flow system included editors who reviewed the content prior to distribution, thus assigning the responsibility to those who subscribe to a set of industry standards and laws set by their governments. For the most part, citizenry understood the obligations of the mass media and relied on the information to the degree in which the information was accountable to the people. However, the Internet, and its open platform, has shifted the flow of information to a new model—where anyone with access to technology, has access to reach the masses, with no accountability to anyone, thus opening the door for legal debate around a plethora of issues with the intent of expanding, limiting or controlling access to information to the masses, including children.

Article 17 does not grant children an absolute right, as a wide range of information is accessible to children, much of it not appropriate for the competence of the child, and information exists that may impart negative influences in their intellectual growth. Within Article 17, the qualifying statements that the information available to children should also be *'aimed at the promotion of his or her social, spiritual and moral well being, and physical and mental health...(through) the encouragement of the mass media to disseminate material...in accordance with the spirit of Article 29.'* The media run by the journalism industry would not see their role as creating a positive or negative impact on society, but as to provide accurate and objective information that allows children to develop into an informed and respectful citizenry. However, the media run by the entertainment industry would likely see their responsibility to produce content that people will buy, and governments may see their role in dissemination of information as to create national support of domestic policies. Who then, has the responsibility of *promoting* the *social, spiritual and moral well-being, and physical and mental health* of children, and how can this be encouraged?

Because freedom of speech is highly regarded in open societies, children have access to a wide variety of information. Society relies on a series of accountability systems to monitor information disseminated and additional monitoring for information available to children. In more authoritarian societies, the media still plays a vital role, however, while there may exist many *media outlets*, the variety of *sources of content* is often limited, therefore restricting the free flow of information and ideas.

'Mass Media' and 'dissemination of information' are terms that are often misunderstood or misused in the context of the law and general population. Mass distribution of information is available to anyone with a printing press, transmitter or Internet access, but the receipt and understanding of it is not guaranteed. Information must also be *received and processed.*

The communication model is a simple one, it requires three elements: a sender, a receiver and a delivery mechanism. If someone has something to say, it is vital that the message is *heard and understood,* otherwise the communication cycle is not complete. The delivery mechanisms available to children are limited and often require a high-level of skill or financial means in order to access them effectively. An illiterate child who lives in poverty without financial or technical resources is further limited in their access to information.

The assurance that a diversity of mass media sources exists in each State is the completion of the communication cycle necessary to create an informed citizenry, one that can decipher multiple messages and make thoughtful decisions based on reliable data.

It is not unusual to hear people say that children need *reliable* information, and sometimes that they have the 'right' to it. This implies that the creator or disseminator of the communication has a duty, moral or legal, to follow certain standards about checking facts, and being fair in the presentation of facts and viewpoints. But the situation is even more complicated than that. Children have to be able to understand information, and have the values, self-control, and other things that are needed to use information wisely. That is a lot of responsibility for a child to hold, and, as important as these matters are, they are not part of Article 17. This Commentary will examine the many industries that develop and distribute mass information to children and the processes that have been put into place by each of them to develop content that will be understood by the child and accepted by the parent or adult who allows the child to access it.

The term media has many interpretations—and as many motivating factors for creating a message to or from children. The term *'media literacy'* has evolved in a necessary effort to assist a consumer of content in determining its reliability, by disclosing the source of its content.

Access to a Diversity of Mass Media Sources is a simple article, aimed at providing a group right to all children—that they have many mass media sources from which to obtain information and materials. However, the misinterpretations of the article have led to confusion from those who have the responsibility to uphold it, due to assumptions made when creating the Reporting Guidelines. This commentary will provide a new, and finally, accurate interpretation of Article 17.

CHAPTER TWO

COMPARISON WITH RELATED HUMAN RIGHTS PROVISIONS

Article 17 of the CRC is unique. There is no counterpart in other global or regional human rights treaties, or national constitutions, or (as far as we know) national legislation. But it is closely related to freedom of expression, a right that is found in the CRC (Article 13), in other treaties, and in most constitutions in the world.

As will be seen in Chapter Three, the essence of Article 17 is diversity in mass media sources: the State has a duty to make sure that children and adolescents have a diversity of mass media sources to choose from. That is to say, the State must ensure access to a variety of producers and disseminators of movies, television and radio programs, books, magazines, the Internet, and other mass media communications. Moreover, Article 17 is a 'group right,' in contrast to most of the other provisions in Part I of the CRC (Articles 1 to 41), which are individually held rights.

The duty to ensure a diversity of mass media sources is often confused with the individually held right that is commonly, but erroneously, referred to as the 'right to freedom of expression,' or just 'freedom of expression,' or the 'right of free speech.'

2.1. *Freedom of Expression Is Made Up of Two Different Rights*

The right to expression in the CRC (Article 13) is nearly identical in wording to the right in the International Covenant on Civil and Political Rights (Article 19). Since the Covenant applies to all human beings, this right to freedom of expression will be used for comparisons. Article 19 of the CCPR says, in part:

2. Everyone shall have the right to *freedom of expression*; this right shall include freedom to seek, *receive* and *impart* information and ideas of all kinds, regardless of frontiers, either orally, in writing or in print, in the form of art or through any other media of his choice.
3. The exercise of the rights provided for in paragraph 2 carries with it special duties and responsibilities. It may therefore be subject to certain restrictions, but these shall only be such as are provided by law and are necessary:

(a) For respect of the rights or reputations of others;
(b) For the protection of national security or of public order (*ordre public*), or of public health or morals.

The first thing to note is that freedom of expression in paragraph 19(2) is an individually held right: every human being possesses the right on a personal or individual basis, as indicated by the word, 'Everyone.'

The second important thing is that 'the right to freedom of expression' is a misnomer. Article 19(2) actually contains two different, but intimately connected, rights: the right to *impart*—to express—a communication, and the right to *receive* a communication. There is no perfect way to capture these two rights in a single term, but 'freedom of communication' comes close: a person has a right communicate to others, and a right to receive another's communication.

These two rights are illustrated in the figure below:

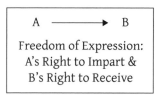

Figure 1

Under the CCPR, only human beings are rights holders. When *A* is a human being, *A* has a right to communicate to any kind of *B* (i.e., an individual human being, a group of people, people in general, or a 'legal person' such a corporation or the State). And when *B* is a human being, *B* has a right to receive communications from any source *A* (i.e., another human being, a group of people, or a legal person).[1]

The third important point is that the two rights are not absolute since they can be limited under paragraph (3). In fact, paragraphs (2) and (3) are competing principles, and they must be balanced against each other before one can determine what any given, real-life right-holder is legally entitled to express, or

---

[1] For simplicity, we have not discussed the right to seek communications. This right seems to be inherent in the right to receive communications because seeking is usually a necessary operational step in receiving. Likewise, seeking to impart is an inherent step in impacting a communication. An author seeks a reader; a staff journalist seeks an editor's approval; a youngster who mails a birthday card to a friend seeks the service of the post office to deliver the card.

to receive, in any given case. The resolution of the conflict between the two principles is determined by some type of a reasonableness (or proportionality) test, and the final decision will ultimately hinge upon value judgments, which are subjective. To put it another way, freedom to impart and freedom to receive are 'negative liberty' rights: the right to be free from unreasonable interference in sending or receiving communications, with reasonableness being determined by reference to the criteria laid down in paragraph (3).[2]

2.2. *The Duty to Ensure a Diversity in Mass Media Sources*

The essence of Article 17 of the CRC is the duty to ensure that young people have a diversity of mass media *As* to choose from. Boys and girls cannot receive communications from a media source *A* if the source does not exist, and they cannot receive a diversity of communications, or choose from a diversity of media sources, unless there is a variety of mass media *As* available to them.

For instance, if there is only one television channel, young people will not have a variety in dissemination sources; and if the only book publisher in the country is the State-own publisher of schoolbooks, there will be no diversity in the production sources within the country. The lack of variety in the sources will tend to mean a lack of diversity in the content of the communications that are available to young people, and a lack of diversity in content will limit the benefits they can receive from television and books, and it will deprive them of choices. The aim of Article 17 is to increase the benefits that adolescents and children can obtain from the mass media by ensuring a diversity in sources of books, newspapers, television programs, music, and other mediums of mass communication.

---

[2] For a helpful way to conceptualize human rights, see Bruce Abramson, *Article 2: The Right of Non-Discrimination* (Martinus Nijhoff, Leiden, Boston, 2008). Like most human rights, freedom of expression exists at two levels: the abstract and the concrete. At the abstract level, the right is what is contained in the text of paragraph (2) of Article 17. Everyone has this right at all times, places, and circumstances. But a right cannot be exercised at the abstract level; it is only enjoyed in real-life, concrete situations. At the concrete level, the right is what any given person is legally entitled to enjoy any given situation, and it is the result of the balancing of the paragraphs (2) and (3) in that situation. At the concrete level, freedom of expression will differ over time, place, and circumstance. The author calls this a 'context-dependent right' to distinguish it from 'absolute rights' (like freedom of opinion and freedom from torture): exercise of a context-dependent right requires balancing decisions, which are based on all relevant factors and ultimately determined by value judgments, while exercise of an absolute right does not. Ibid., 33–37.

The essence of Article 17 is illustrated in the figure below:

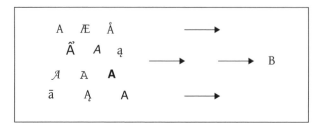

Figure 2

B is the individual adolescent or child. The various *A*s are mass media sources. The primary duty in Article 17 is for the State to make sure that young people in the country have a variety of *A*s from which to choose.

There are two main kinds of sources of communications in the mass media industry: producers and disseminators. Examples of producers would be authors of books, and composers of music. The materials they create are delivered to the public by disseminators. Mass media disseminators include radio stations and CD stores for music, and bookstores and libraries for books. The sources of mass media communications are typically legal persons (e.g., corporations), or governmental entities, like public libraries and State-owned radio and television facilities. These legal persons and State entities do not hold human rights under the CRC (or the CCPR).

The differences between freedom of expression and Article 17 of the CRC are clear. *Freedom of expression* is made up of two reciprocal rights: the right to send, and the right to receive, communications. Every young person under the CRC, and every human being under the CCPR, has a right to receive mass media communications under their right to freedom of expression. (This is represented by *B* in Figures 1 and 2.) Freedom of expression is a negative liberty right that is held by individuals. By contrast, *Article 17* of the CRC imposes a duty on the State to make sure that there are a variety of mass media sources. (The diversity is represented by the variety of *A*s in Figure 2.) Article 17 is not an individually held right: it is a positive duty placed on the State to ensure the existence of diversity in mass media sources. In common parlance, it can be called a collective or group right.

The comparison can be sharpened by saying what Article 17 is not about. First, it is not about the right of mass media sources to create or disseminate communications to young people. (Corporations and the State do not hold human rights under the human rights treaties created through the United Nations. However, legal persons could hold rights to send and receive communications under national laws and regional human rights treaties.) Second, Article 17 is not about the right, or the duty, of the State to censor the content of mass media material to safeguard adolescents and children. It is true that Article 17 requires the State to encourage the privately owned media industry to develop guidelines to protect young people, but it does not impose a duty on the State to protect young people. Instead, *duties to protect* young people from harmful mass media content come under other provisions of the CRC, like the duty to 'protect the child against all other forms of exploitation prejudicial to any aspects of the child's welfare' (Article 30), and the all-encompassing duty to ensure the healthy development of the child (under the mega-right, Article 6). And the State's *right to censor*, under human rights law, comes from the paragraphs that subject freedom of expression to some sort of a balancing test (i.e., Article 19(3) of the CCPR, and Article 13(2) of the CRC.) And third, it is not about the right of adolescents and children to receive mass media communications; the right to receive a communication comes from the right to freedom of expression (Article 19 of the CCPR, and Article 13 of the CRC).

There is a considerable amount of confusion about Article 17 in the children's rights literature. The confusion usually springs from a widespread under-appreciation of the uniqueness of the Article; in particular, the failure to distinguish between the *right to receive* a communication, which is part of freedom of expression, and the *duty of the State* to make sure that young people have a *diversity of mass media sources* from which to choose.

For instance, one publication summarizes Article 17 this way: 'You have the right to collect information from radios, newspapers, television, books, etc. from all around the world. Adults should make sure that you get information you can understand.'[3] As will be seen in the next chapter on the scope of Article 17, this paraphrase does not come close to explaining the content of the Article. The Commentary will also discuss, among other things, some of the reasons for this confusion (the primary cause being the Reporting Guidelines of the CRC Committee), and will show how the confusion has deprived the public of information about what States are doing to realize Article 17.

---

[3] UNICEF, 'Convention on the Rights of the Child,' YMCA World (World Alliance of YMCAs, No. 4, Dec., 2001).

CHAPTER THREE

SCOPE OF ARTICLE 17

To define the scope of a legal duty is to state the contents of the duty, or its meaning or elements. This section will apply the rules of treaty interpretation to determine the legal meaning of Article 17. The chapter concludes that the Article is made up of three duties.

The State's primary obligation is to make sure that adolescents and children have a diversity of mass media sources from which to choose. The secondary duty is to make sure that some of these sources are producing materials that are beneficial to young people. The third duty is actually a series of obligations that are framed in terms of 'encouraging' other actors to produce and distribute material that will promote the well-being of children and adolescents.

These duties are based on the same understanding: the mass media—television, radio, books, magazines, newspapers, and so forth—has a tremendous capacity to promote the well-being of children and adolescents. This understanding has its greatest force in the primary duty, which requires the State to expand the role of mass media in the lives of young people. But, there is also a dark side to the mass media. The materials that sometimes come to youngsters through the media can hurt them, and can also harm society at large. The delegates that created Article 17 recognized this harmful potential, but made a policy decision not to address it in this Article, except in a very limited way. This means that the State's duty to protect youngsters from harmful affects of mass media, are outside of the scope of the Article.

When taking a holistic perspective on the CRC, it must also include the fact that the media has the potential to harm young people. As the State Party and civil society actors take steps to expand the role of mass media in the lives of CRC right-holders, the dangers must also be anticipated, and measures to eliminate or minimize the harm must be included. In order to ensure that Article 17 is viewed from a holistic perspective, this commentary will address some of the negative aspects of mass media in the last chapter.

3.1. *The Rules of Interpretation*

This commentary will apply the rules in the Vienna Convention on the Law of Treaties to interpret Article 17. In particular, we will use what is sometimes called the ordinary meaning rule: 'A treaty shall be interpreted [a] in good faith [b] in accordance with the ordinary meaning to be given to the terms of the treaty [c] in their context and [d] in light of its object and purpose' (brackets added).[4]

3.2. *The First Sentence of Article 17*

Article 17 is made up of two sentences. The first sentence reads:

> [1.] [A] States Parties recognize the important function performed by the mass media and
> [B] shall ensure that the child has access to information and material from a diversity of national and international sources,
> [C] especially those aimed at the promotion of his or her social, spiritual and moral well-being and physical and mental health. (Brackets and indentation added.)

This one sentence is made up of three clauses, and it contains a surprising number of legal questions. All of the major legal issues will be addressed by examining the sentence clause by clause.

3.2.1   *Clause-by-Clause Analysis*

[A] *'States Parties recognize the important function performed by the mass media...'*

This clause raises two interpretation questions. First, is it a substantive clause? That is to say, does it impose any obligations on the State, or does it qualify or limit any obligations?

There should be no doubt that the clause is not substantive. It is in the nature of a preamble, and, like the preambular paragraphs that precede Article 1 of the CRC, it neither creates nor limits a State's duties. At most, a preambular statement can give insight into the framers' point of view or objective in creating the ensuing obligations, in which case it might help to resolve disputes over an interpretation.[5]

---

[4] Article 31(1) of the VCLT, 1155 UNTS 331 (1969; in force 1980).
[5] The Working Group recognized that the clause was a preamble, and amended the sentence. Office of the United Nations High Commissioner for Human Rights, *Legislative History of the Convention on the Rights of the Child* (New York/Geneva, United Nations, 2007), p. 486 (para. 57 of the UN records). The *Legislative History* is available on-line at www.ohchr.org. Despite the amendment, the first sentence was still not good legal drafting. A preamble should not be a mere clause in the sentence that imposes a duty. It should be a full sentence, and placed in a separate paragraph, as in Article 23(1) (children with disabilities). As will be seen throughout the legal

The preamble-like clause recognizes a fact—that mass media performs an important function—but it does not say what that function is. To understand the States' obligations in Article 17, the interpretation starts by identifying why mass media is important to children and adolescents. A good source for understanding what the framers of the CRC probably had in mind is the report of the International Commission for the Study of Communication Problem, a prestigious body set up by UNESCO to study and make recommendations for global action pertaining to mass media and other forms of communication. The landmark study is popularly known 'MacBride Report' in honor of the Commission's president, Sean MacBride, winner of the Nobel Peace Prize. The Report was published in 1980, just as the process of creating the CRC got underway.[6]

The MacBride Report identified the many ways that communication is important to the well-being of individuals: (i) Entertainment for pleasure and recreation; (ii) Education; (iii) Information for decision-making, including the exercise of rights; (iv) Motivation, which includes the stimulation of personal choices and aspirations; (v) Debate and discussion, as when people exchange facts and clarify viewpoints; (vi) Socialization, so individuals can become effective members of society; (vii) Integration of the person into the world community, as when one learns about and understands peoples of other countries and cultures, and (viii) Cultural promotion, as in the preservation of a heritage and the promotion of national and other identities.[7]

All of these benefits of communication in general come from the mass media in particular, and they are enjoyed by children and adolescents as well as adults, although the benefits can differ depending on age, especially for very young children. In addition to these mostly future-oriented, utilitarian benefits, included are (ix) personal autonomy: the sheer joy that an adolescent or child feels when making his or her own choice about what to read, watch, and listen to, the sheer pleasure of being able to act upon one's own intuition of what will make a meaningful experience in the here-and-now.

The preamblular clause indicates that the overall purpose of the Article is to secure the benefits of the mass media to young people, and, by keeping in mind the multiple ways that the media contributes to immediate well-being and long term development of young people, Article 17 is interpreted to maximize the actual receipt of those benefits.

---

analysis, the craftsmanship in writing Article 17 was not up to the prevailing standards in UN human rights treaties.

[6] International Commission for the Study of Communication Problems, *Many Voices, One World: Towards a new and more efficient world information and communication order* (Kogan Page, London/Unipub, New York/UNESCO, Paris, no date 1980). Hereafter, *MacBride Report*.

[7] Ibid., p. 14. The categories in the Report are a bit different, but the list in the main text includes all the functions that the Report identified.

'mass media'

Mass media has to be interpreted because it has two ordinary meanings. It can refer to a 'means of mass communication,' such as airwaves (the means for radio, television, and satellites), and print (for newspapers, books, and posters).[8] And it can also mean the 'communications industry or profession.'[9] While the context of the preambular clause strongly suggests the second meaning, it must be interpreted in the full context of the entire sentence, not just the first clause.

'States Parties . . . [B] shall ensure that the child has access to information and material from a diversity of national and international sources, . . .'

This clause is the heart of Article 17: it imposes a demanding legal obligation on States Parties, and the key word *sources* interprets that *mass media* refers to the industry, to the businesses and people that provide communications through the airwaves, print and other mediums.

'information and material'

The most basic meaning of *information*, relevant in this context, is a 'collection of facts or data,' or a 'communication of knowledge.'[10] News reports, documentaries, and related forms of journalism would clearly be examples of 'information.' *Materials*, on the other hand, seems to be used here as an all-encompassing word. The mass media industry produces and disseminates a wide variety of communications, and the substance of those communications can be summarized as 'material': soap operas and a production of the Ramayana on television, pop music over the Internet, an animated movie on a DVD, and advertising posters on city buses—everything that the mass media industry communicates is covered by the generic word *material*. 'Information' is just one kind of the material that mass media sources transmit to audiences. (For convenience, *communications* is used as an umbrella word to cover both material and information.)

mass media 'sources'

It's customary to divide the media industry into producers and disseminators of material.[11] For example, movie studios and independent filmmakers are

---

[8] *The American Heritage Dictionary* (4th Ed., Dell Book/Random House, New York, 2001), p. 528.
[9] Ibid.
[10] Ibid., p. 438 (meanings 3 and 4 of the term). In addition to the ordinary meanings, there are term-of-art definitions, such as those found in the fields of information theory and information technology.
[11] *MacBride Report, o.c.* (note 6), at 197.

producers of movies, and the main disseminators are movie theaters, television stations, shops that sell DVDs and videos, and online retailers. And in the book industry, publishing houses are producers, and the disseminators include bookshops, online retailers, libraries, and, for education books, schools. Of course, all of the media industries involve many more components than those listed. Mass media producers and disseminators are virtually always corporations, and they employ an army of creative people; for example, a movie studio will have screenwriters, actors, directors, cameramen, and editors, to name a few. And then there are the 'middle-men' distributors, the advertising industry, and the technology industries. But the traditional division between producers and disseminators is still valid, and both could be considered as 'sources' of mass media communications in ordinary speech. So, for the purposes of Article 17, should *source* be interpreted to mean only disseminators, or only producers, or as referring to both?

Four considerations support reading *sources* as meaning both producers and disseminators. First, producers and disseminators do not exist apart from each other; they are like 'two hands clapping': working together, they become the means by which the efforts of creative people (authors, journalists, singers, artists, and so forth) are transformed into 'mass media,' and communicated to audiences. Second, ensuring diversity of both producers and disseminators will provide more diversity of materials to young people, and the more diverse the communications, the greater the benefits they can receive. Third, since the next sentence of Article 17 speaks of both—e.g., 'Encourage the production and dissemination of children's books,' in paragraph (c)—it is clear the framers had both in mind. And fourth, since the framers chose to use the broad word *source* without limiting it or defining it, it should be given it a broad reading in order to maximize the benefits of the Article.

'shall ensure'

'Shall ensure' is the highest imposition of duty known in human rights law. Some provisions in the CRC have much softer duties, like 'shall pursue,' 'shall take...measures with a view to,' and 'shall seek to promote.'[12] Those softer duties are framed in terms of working towards an end result, but don't require any specified action in the here and now. By contrast, 'shall ensure' in Article 17 requires the State *to make sure* of something in the here and now.

---

[12] Respectively, Article 24(2) (fulfilling the right to health), Article 24(3) (ending harmful traditional practices), and Article 40(3) (setting up a juvenile justice system).

'the child'

Grammarians call *the* a definite article, and it is typically used to identify a specific person or thing (e.g., 'Give the book to the child sitting by the door'). But *the* can be used in several other ways as well.

In the CRC, *the child* is used most often in the sense of 'each (or every) child.'[13] And in some other provisions it means a child that has been referred to previously.[14] But in several places, *the child* is a collective noun, and it means the plural *children*. Here are three examples: The title of the treaty: 'Convention on the Rights of the Child (i.e., Children).'[15] Article 3(1): 'In all actions concerning children... the best interests of the child (i.e., those children) shall be a primary consideration.' And throughout Article 17: 'ensure that the child has access'; 'cultural benefit to the child'; 'the linguistic needs of the child'; and 'protection of the child.' By definition, the mass media produce and disseminate communications to the masses. A movie studio does not make a film for every under-18 year-old in a country, or for any particular young person; a book publisher does not assess the language needs of every youngster in an indigenous group, for instance. *The child* has a plural meaning throughout Article 17.[16]

---

[13] For example: 'the [**every**] child shall be registered immediately after birth...' (CRC, Article 7). We can see the inter-changeability of *the* and *every* by comparing this article to the CCPR: '*Every* child shall be registered immediately after birth...' (CCPR, Article 24(2) (emphasis added)). It means 'every child' because it is a right that every child possess as an individual.

[14] For example: The State shall 'ensure that the adoption of **a** child is authorized...[and] is permissible in view of the [**that**] child's status concerning parents...' (Article 21(a)); and 'unless it is considered not to be in the best interests of the [**that**] child...' (Art. 40(2)(b)(iii)). In usages like these, the person or persons who are the subject of the statement have been identified earlier in the sentence, so *the child* is a reference back to those particular individuals, and the term could be replaced by *that child, such a child,* or *the child in question.*

[15] Compare to the title, 'Convention on the Elimination of All Forms of Discrimination Against Women.' Why didn't the framers write 'the Woman' instead of 'Women'? From the 1960s, it has been considered offensive to use collective nouns for demographic groups of people, so that 'the woman,' 'the African,' and so forth are now taboo. Only 'the child' remains acceptable. Bruce Abramson, 'The Invisibility of Children and Adolescents,' in: E. Verhellen (ed.), *Monitoring Children's Rights* (Kluwer Law International, The Hague, 1996), pp. 395–396.

[16] The framers of the CRC used the plural *children* more than twenty times, e.g., Article 3(1) & (3), and Article 18(2) & (3), and in several references, 'Declaration on the Protection of Women and Children in Emergency and Armed Conflict' (preamble, para. ten), and 'United Nations Children's Fund' (Article 45(a)).

Using *the child* in Article 17 was a drafting error because it conflicts with the Convention's definition. In its ordinary meaning, *child* refers to a person under the age of puberty, or at most under the age of 15 years. Article 1 creates a legal fiction, or term-of-art, because it extends *child* to include adolescents up to 18 years. 'The Invisibility of Children and Adolescents,' *o.c.* (note 15), pp. 397–398. But if one plugs the term-of-art meaning into Article 17, the result is nonsense: e.g., 'ensure that [every human being under the age of 18 years] has access to' mass media communications. Babies in the pre-natal and post-natal periods are not consumers of mass media. The framers should have used the plural *children*, referring in a generalized way to the entire demographic group,

So when Article 17 says that the State 'shall ensure that the child [i.e., children] has [have] access,' it does not mean the authorities have to take individualized action for each person under 18 years of age. It is a generalized duty to ensure that a large group of people—all children and adolescents—have access.

'access to information and material from a diversity of national and international sources'

This is the most difficult part of the legal interpretation. It is difficult because the sentence is ambiguous as to the primary object or focus of *access to*: (i) 'Ensure access to *communications* (which come from a diversity of mass media sources)'; or (ii) 'Ensure access to a *diversity of mass media sources* (which provide the communications).' The two readings result in the same obligations for the State; what is different is where our primary attention goes.

There are two interconnected dangers with putting the primary focus on the communications, under the first reading. It can lead to seeing the Article in terms of the right to receive communications, which is part of the right of expression and not Article 17. And it can result in downplaying, or even ignoring, the duty to ensure that there is a diversity of mass media sources. The second reading, by contrast, keeps all aspects of the duty in mind. This is because 'ensuring access to a diversity of mass media sources' inherently entails ensuring that young people have access to the communications coming from those sources: access to the sources means access to their communications.

The second reading is viewed as containing two parts: the State must ensure that a diversity of sources *exists*, and it must ensure that it exists in such a way that the communications are *available* to young people. When television stations and libraries exist in the capital, but do not extend to the rural areas, then these sources exist in the nation, but are not available to those who live outside the city. So the duty is not just to ensure that a diversity of mass media sources exist, but that their communications are in fact available to young people throughout the nation. The specific sources available in one locality can be different from what is available in other places, since the Article does not call for uniformity (and uniformity would be impossible as a practical matter). The duty is a generalized one: the State has to make sure that a *diversity* of sources is *available* to young people:

---

without concern with individualization. The technical review of the draft CRC should have caught the drafting error. Apparently the UNICEF reviewers were so fixated on 'gender neutrality'—making sure that the singular *child* was not paired with the masculine pronoun *his*—that they were not able to read the text for sense—and therefore could not see when *the child* has a plural meaning—, or to catch the absurdity resulting from the legal fiction in this context. *Legislative History*, *o.c.* (note 5), p. 490 (sec. D.2 of the *History*).

that the group has access to a diversity of sources, which inherently means having access to the communications that come from those diverse sources.

It is important to make the distinction between 'access' and 'accessible.' The word *accessible* contains the idea of relative ease in attaining the object. This element is made clear in dictionary definitions. (E.g., 'able to be easily obtained or used.')[17] But the word in Article 17 is *access*, and it has two ordinary meanings that need to be considered in this context: 'A means of approaching, entering, exiting, or making use of; passage,' and 'The right to approach, enter, exit, or make use of.'[18] Neither of these usages gives a clear idea of what the State must do in the context of Article 17; in particular, neither meaning contains the idea that a person can easily obtain the object.[19]

So 'access' is a much more generalized word than 'accessible,' which makes sense in Article 17: to 'ensure' that the large demographic group 'children,' whose members are highly diverse in personal characteristics and widely dispersed geographically, have 'access' to communications from a 'diversity' of sources falling under the broad heading of 'mass media,' is a generalized legal duty. It would not require the State make sure that every young person actually receives communications from diverse sources. (That could require the State the force people to receive material against their will, depriving them of freedom of choice.) And it would not require the State to make sure that every young person can 'gain access,' as he or she chooses, to books, CDs, movies, and other mass communications, or to make them 'accessible' or 'affordable.' (That could require the State to give out free radios, or to force private businesses to hand out free radios, when children and their parents cannot afford to buy them.)

---

[17] *Oxford Dictionary of English* (2nd Ed., revised, Oxford Univ. Press, Oxford, 2005), p. 9. See also, *The American Heritage Dictionary of the English Language* (3rd ed., Houghton Mifflin Co., Boston/New York/London, 1992), p. 10. The Committee on Economic, Social and Cultural Rights uses *accessibility* to refer to relative easy in obtaining social goods and services. E.g., 'safe reach' and 'reasonably convenient,' in 'General Comment No. 13: The Right to Education,' para. 6(b) (under 'Physical accessibility'), UN Doc. HRI/GEN/1/Rev.8 (2006), p. 73.

[18] *The American Heritage Dictionary of the English Language* (3rd Ed., Houghton Mifflin Co., Boston/New York/London, 1992), p. 10 (meanings 1 and 3). While the second clause was introduced by the United States at the Working Group, so that the American usages would probably be the best guide to the intentions, the British usages are the same: 'the means or opportunity to approach or enter a place'; 'the right or opportunity to use or benefit from something.' *Oxford Dictionary of English, o.c.* (note 17), p. 9 (meaning 1).

[19] Confusion about the meaning of *access* is increased because it is often used figuratively, especially as a blanket word when the speaker has no clear meaning in mind ('access to feelings,' 'access to thoughts,' 'access to love'), and in ways contrary to the norms of good English; see, e.g., *American Heritage Dictionary*, previous note. And the fuzziness of meaning is convenient in political contexts when expanding claims through ambiguity can be advantageous (e.g., 'access to rights,' and expanding 'access to courts' to 'access to justice'), which can lead to the blurring of the distinction between *access* and *accessibility*.

Instead, the duty is to ensure that a diversity of mass media sources are generally available. If radio stations serve only city dwellers, then this medium would not be available to the people who live in the countryside. Article 17 would then require the State to expand radio services so that programs are available to young people throughout the nation.

So the duty to ensure access to a diversity of mass media sources is not an extreme duty, but it is still a tough duty. For instance, some of the mediums of communication require complex and expensive infrastructures, like satellite systems and television stations. The economies in many countries are not strong enough for these needs to be filled by private enterprise alone, and where this is the case, the State itself will probably not have the money to build and run these facilities. Many States will therefore have to obtain international and regional assistance in order to fulfill their duties under Article 17. (The framers addressed this to a limited extent in Article 17: the State shall 'encourage international cooperation in the production, exchange and dissemination' of mass media communications, in paragraph (b) in the second sentence.)[20]

'a diversity' of mass media sources

Diversity means 'variety':[21] that within a set of things, the members of the set belong to different categories. Diversity in content is, of course, what is ultimately desired: people benefit when they have a wide variety of information, ideas, viewpoints, analysis, and experiences through comedy, drama, adventure, music, and other art forms. The ultimate aim of Article 17 is to extend the benefits of the mass media to young people, and the greater the variety in the content of the materials available, the richer the opportunities for them to benefit.

There are two ways for a State to ensure that the public has a variety of content. (i) The State can directly regulate the material that is produced and disseminated. This route raises serious concerns about State interference into people's lives, not to mention the severe financial and administrative burdens that such regulation would put on the government. It is highly unlikely that the framers of the CRC would have chosen this approach. Or (ii), the State can ensure that there is diversity among the producers and disseminators of mass media. Diversity in sources will lead, in the natural course of events, to greater diversity in content, while

---

[20] The enormous challenges of building and running these infrastructures, and the need for assistance and partnerships, is discussed in *MacBride Report, o.c.* (note 6), pp. 213–222. Moreover, for newspapers, magazines, and television and movie production, many developed states find it necessary to give subsides to keep these industries alive. Ibid., pp. 99–103. For a chart showing how thirteen European states give fourteen kinds of subsides to newspapers, see Ibid., p. 101.

[21] *The American Heritage Dictionary* (4th Ed.), *o.c.* (note 18), p. 252.

avoiding direct State regulation of the content itself. This is the strategy that the framers of Article 17 adopted.[22]

But what does 'diversity in sources' mean? There are many possible ways to classify producers and disseminators of mass media, so before diversity of sources can be discussed, they must be categorized.

It has become common practice to talk about core obligations and minimum standards of human rights treaties. Article 17 requires the State to ensure access to a diversity of mass media sources, so in interpreting this duty, the core ways to judge whether there is variety has to be defined. The text of the Article, together with common sense, backed up by the MacBride Report, produce four classifications of most concern. These four classifications should be included in the core obligations pertaining to 'diversity' of mass media sources.

(i) *Ownership*

One of the most obvious ways to judge diversity is by ownership. In fact, the MacBride Report was deeply concerned about the '[c]oncentration of ownership in fewer and fewer hands.' Owners control the communications that their companies produce and disseminate, and over-concentration will tend to restrict diversity of sources, and thus diminish the variety in content.[23]

In some countries, private companies either hold monopolies or exercise a dominance that stifles other producers and disseminators.[24] On top of this, there

---

[22] The text of the Article does not specifically tell us that that was the thinking behind framing the duty in terms of diversity of sources, but the logic of this strategy is so compelling that we are justified in inferring that that was the reasoning, and this conclusion is supported by the legislative records. *Legislative History, o.c.* (note 5), p. 483 (sec. 7(a) of the *History*) and p. 485 (para. 53 of the UN records). In particular, the clause was introduced by the United States, which explained that the delegates 'should take into account the concerns of States where the private sector was involved in the mass media and that it was not possible or desirable for the State to ensure or guarantee anything in that field.' Ibid., p. 485 (para. 53 of the UN records).

Censorship happens when the state eliminates a communication with X content because it dislikes those kind of messages. Diversity in sources is the existence of sources A, B, C, etc. There can still be diversity in sources even though the state forbids them to communicate X. but problems can arise. For instance, a state might use 'ensuring diversity of sources' as an excuse to censor when it allocates licenses for finite resources like radio frequencies: if it denies a license to a source that deals in X messages and gives it to a source dealing in Y messages, and does this because it wants to suppress X, then this would be censorship.

[23] 'Concentration of ownership in fewer and fewer hands is causing anxiety in many countries today. Industrialization has tended to stimulate a concentration in the communication sector through the formation of oligopolies and monopolies in the gathering, storing, and dissemination of information.' *MacBride Report, o.c.* (note 6), p. 104. See also, Ibid., at pp. 22, 23 note (1), and 96–111.

[24] 'For example, in some countries, as many as five television channels are operated by a single company; in some others, newspaper and broadcasting systems may be under the same ownership; in other situations, the benefits of diversity are lost when several media under the same ownership speak with the same voice.' Ibid., p. 23, footnote (1).

is a trend in vertical and horizontal integration, the formation of multi-media conglomerates, and ownership of media sources by giant companies that also control completely unrelated businesses (like car manufacturing, hotel chains, and dog food).[25] The concern with these trends is at least two fold. One worry is that decisions about content will be increasingly determined by profit alone, without being tempered by the traditional constraints of a social conscience. Another concern is these mega-business have so much power that they can eliminate or restrict the competition whenever they like.

In some other countries, the State has a monopoly on radio, television, and other mediums. This can happen when the State has ideological motivations for controlling the communications that the public receives.[26] A State monopoly can also happen by default, when the economy cannot support privately owned mass media sources, which depend mainly on advertising or user-fees.[27] In either case, the public has fewer sources to choose from, which means less information and materials, and less variety in the content.

(ii) *Origins of the Sources*

The MacBride Report was also concerned about diversity in the origins, or the geo-political locations, of the mass media sources. One problem is 'one way information flows,' especially when the Western entertainment saturates developing countries.[28] This can restrict the production of indigenous materials, undermine national and ethnic values and ways of life, and deprive people in the West of the benefits of receiving the news, entertainment, culture, and analysis from unfamiliar parts of the world.[29] Moreover, worries about 'cultural imperialism,' 'cultural alienation,' and the eroding of national identity are not confined to developing countries. Some Western States put limits on foreign programs that can be shown on television and the pop music played over the radio. Another problem is when a State restricts communications from abroad in order to insolate the people from outside news, analysis, entertainment, and cultural perspectives.[30]

---

[25] Ibid., p. 104.
[26] Ibid., pp. 20–21.
[27] Ibid., pp. 100–103.
[28] Ibid., pp. 145–149.
[29] Ibid., pp. 159–164.
[30] Complaints about Western domination of the media go beyond the contents of the materials and include the control of technology and the global systems of telecommunications. In his book, *Global Communication: Theories, Stakeholder, and Trends*, Thomas L. McPhail analyses what he calls 'electronic colonialism': 'the dependent relationship of poorer regions on the post industrial nations caused and established by the importation of communication hardware and foreign-produced software, along with engineers, technicians, and related information protocols, that establish a set of foreign norms, values, and expectations that, to varying degrees, alter domestic cultures, languages, habits, values and the socialization process itself.' Ibid., p. 18.

The framers of Article 17 were so concerned about diversity in origins that they expressly included it in two places: 'diversity of national and international sources', and 'diversity of cultural, national, and international sources' (in paragraph (b) of the second sentence). As for international sources, it can be taken it a step further and classified according to regions of the world.[31]

(iii) *Product Categories: Age-Groups and Subject Matter*
Another important way to classify source is by the product categories of the materials that they produce and disseminate.

The mass media create materials for targeted audiences defined in terms of large-scale demographic groups. The CRC is about one giant demographic group—all human beings under the age of 18 years—and this gigantic group is made up of numerous sub-groups of children and adolescents. In the print industry, for example, publishing houses might deal in children's books (which is mentioned in the second sentence of Article 17, to be discussed below), young adult fiction, teen magazines, or general (adult) fiction.

Sources can also be classified generally by the type of material that they produce. For instance, in the music industry, production companies can specialize in pop, rap, classical, or religious recordings, and publishing houses can deal in magazines or books about Information Technology, fashion, sports, romance fiction, self-help, science or history.

(iv) *Mediums*
The last classification is perhaps the most obvious: variety defined by the mediums of mass communications. Every State should ensure that young people have access to all of the traditional mediums—print (e.g., books, magazines, newspapers), recordings, radio, movies, and television—and to the modern mediums—satellites and the Internet—that disseminate the digitalized forms of the traditional products.

Since all States have communications that come from all of these sources, one could argue that this classification has been overlooked. But the significance of including the mediums under the 'diversity of sources' requirement will become apparent when discussing the singular 'child' to the plural 'children': the State must ensure that a diversity of mass media sources is available to the entire population of young people in the country. This identifies the problem of disparities

---

[31] Professor Jeremy Tunstall has identified four major media regions in the world: Euro-America (which encompasses Latin America); India; China; and the Arab-language region. He also says that domestic media often exists at four levels: national, regional, local, and neighbor nation-states. *The Media Were American* (Oxford University Press, USA, 2007).

in access to mass media communications—the uneven distribution of the various mediums throughout the State, the gaps in the availability of the Internet, television, books, and so forth between different segments of the population. The problem of disparities in access will be discussed in the next section.

Putting all of this together, the duty can be paraphrased as: 'The State has to make sure that children and adolescents throughout all the country have access to communications from a diversity of mass media sources, with 'diversity' being measured by at least four core variables (ownership, origins, product category—age groups and subject matter—and mediums).'

'shall ensure that the child [children] has [have] access'

Once it is recognized that *the child* is a collective noun, and that it means all persons under the age of 18, then the concern about 'ensuring access' becomes a concern about disparities in access between groups of young people. The duty to ensue access becomes a duty to reduce or eliminate the disparities in availability.

Disparities in Access

The starting place for creating measures to correct the imbalances is to identify which groups of young people who do not have access to the various sources, and the reasons for the unevenness. There are three problems that frequently cause disparities in access. (i) Geographical limits to distribution. (E.g., the radio and television stations in the capital city do not extend to rural areas; there are no satellite-reception stations in the mountain areas; there is no electricity in a remote area so people cannot operate televisions and computers for the Internet.) (ii) Language. (E.g., the material is not translated into, or is not originally created in, the language of a national language group or immigrant group.) (The framers addressed this to a limited degree in paragraph (d) in the second sentence.) And, (iii) Disability. (E.g., books and magazines are not rendered into Braille or into audio versions for the blind and visually impaired, and television programs and movies are not subtitled for the deaf and hearing impaired.)

Disparities in Accessibility and in Attainments

When a holistic perspective is taken, disparities in access to the mass media are only one concern. *Disparities in accessibility* must also be addressed. When young people have the same wants or needs, but some are able to obtain satisfaction when they choose to while others cannot, then 'barriers' to obtainment raise questions about fairness, and to debates about when the State should intervene to make it easier to obtain goods and services. In addition, the holistic perspective requires attention to *disparities in attainments*. The ultimate objective of the CRC is to promote the human dignity, or the overall well-being, of everyone under 18, or, as the 'mega-right' Article 6 puts it, to ensure each youngster's 'survival and [healthy] development' to 'the maximum extent possible.' While the notions of access and accessibility involve possibilities or potentials, attainment is about whether people are actually getting what they need in order to achieve that end-objective.

Attention to unevenness in accessibility and in attainments adds several more problems to the three mentioned above: (iv) Illiteracy and lack of education. (E.g., people cannot read books; their education is insufficient to follow discussions on the radio; they cannot understand the operating instructions for communication technologies.) And (v), Economics. (E.g., the young person or the youngster's family cannot afford to pay for books, a television, or a computer and access to the Internet.)

'...[C] especially those aimed at the promotion of his or her social, spiritual and moral well-being and physical and mental health.'

The primary duty is neutral as to the social value of the communications: the obligation is to make sure there is a diversity of mass media sources. This last clause is concerned with sources classified in terms of a particular type of content: sources that produce or disseminate material *aimed at the promotion of well-being* of young people. There are several important points about the last clause.

The word *especially* requires the State to make sure that, among the diversity of sources, there are some that produce beneficial material of the kind described in the 'especially...' clause. In the graphic of the diverse *As* communicating to *B* (Figure 2), the 'especially...' clause requires the State to make sure that there are *As* that produce material that is beneficial to children and adolescents. In other words, the first sentence imposes two duties. The primary duty is to ensure access to diverse mass media sources, and the secondary duty is to ensure that, within this diversity, there are producers and disseminators of material designed to be beneficial to minors.[32]

The word *especially* implies several things. For one, it implies priority in action: when the State makes plans for increasing the diversity of sources, it should give preference to measures that will increase the number of sources that generate or

---

[32] The clause contains a duty to ensure that there are sources that aim to promote the spiritual well-being of children. This could be important in several scenarios. For instance, if a State said that it must take a strict 'secular' approach to the media, it would still have to ensure there were sources dealing in religious materials. Or if a State has a one-religion policy, it would still have to allow diversity among sources dealing in religious communications. See section 3.2.2 below on the implied standard of reasonableness.

disseminate beneficial material. For another, 'beneficial programs' could serve as a benchmark or indicator of diversity. To give an illustration, if television stations are not showing many beneficial programs, such as dramas with characters who display admirable qualities like courage and compassion, or that teach about wildlife, science, and health to children, then there would be insufficient diversity in television sources. The State would then need to take action to increase the number of producers that create quality programming for young people.

And finally, *especially* implies that, among the diverse media sources, some will disseminate material that does *not promote* the well-being of young people. Some of this non-beneficial material will be harmless. (Mindless cartoons on television might be an example. While one could argue that such cartoons do not promote well-being, children still enjoy watching them, and that can be a sufficient justification for showing them. And parents like them because cartoons kept the children quiet, allowing the parents to get rest or get their cores done, which in turns contributes to order and harmony of the home.) But other material will be controversial, and some of it might clearly be harmful to children or teenagers. What is important to note is that nothing in the first sentence, including the 'especially...' clause, authorizes or requires State censorship of the content of the material being disseminated, whether to weed out 'junk' entertainment or to safeguard young people from harmful material.

This realization makes some serious questions spring to mind. Since the first sentence allows non-beneficial material, how does Article 17 address the protection of adolescents and children? How does the CRC, and human rights overall, safeguard young people from media content that could hurt them? This Commentary has already spoken on these questions, and it will return to them in later sections, but the answer can be summarized in a single sentence: Article 17 is not about State censorship of the content of the communications sent out by mass media: Article 17 neither requires nor authorizes censorship: protection from harmful content must be handled under other Articles of the CRC, and under the provisions of other treaties and national law.

3.2.2   *The Implied 'Reasonableness' Element Pertaining to the Standard of the Duty*

The first sentence imposes a strict duty to establish and maintain a certain state of affairs: States Parties 'shall ensure' the availability of 'a diversity' of mass media sources of communications. There is no ambiguity about *diversity*: it means 'a variety.' But there is considerable uncertainty about how the duty should be applied to particular situations: How much variety is required? How is it determined a particular State has enough diversity in producers and disseminators to satisfy the 'shall ensure...' clause?

The law—whether international, regional, or national—has a simple solution to problems like this: one reads into the provision some kind of a reasonableness test. Different jurisdictions use different terminology for this; in Europe, for instance, the implied term is often 'proportionality.' But the concept is the same: the performance of the duty is judged by a reasonableness standard.[33] In the first sentence of Article 17, the State has a duty to ensure that there is a *reasonable* diversity of mass media sources, and that within this diversity, there is a reasonable amount of producers and disseminators of materials that are beneficial to adolescents and children.

3.3. *The Second Sentence of Article 17*

The second sentence reads:

> [2.] To this end, States Parties shall:
> (a) Encourage the mass media to disseminate information and material of social and cultural benefit to the child and in accordance with the spirit of Article 29;
> (b) Encourage international co-operation in the production, exchange, and dissemination of such information and material from a diversity of cultural, national, and international sources;
> (c) Encourage the production and dissemination of children's books;
> (d) Encourage the mass media to have particular regard to the linguistic needs of the child who belongs to a minority group or who is indigenous;
> (e) Encourage the development of appropriate guidelines for the protection of the child from information and material injurious to his or her well-being, bearing in mind the provisions of Articles 13 and 18. (Bracketed number added.)

One of the first things that catches the eye is that *mass media* always refers to sources, which is consistent with the interpretation of the same term in the first sentence. Another eye-catcher is that *encourage* is the duty in all of the paragraphs.

---

[33] The principle of proportionality is a reasonableness test. The proportionality principle requires that 'the measure taken bear a *reasonable* relationship to the aim of the measure'; H. Victor Condé, *A Handbook of International Human Rights Terminology*, p. 208 (emphasis added). See also, P. van Dijk, and F. van Hoof, *Theory and Practice of the European Convention on Human Rights* (3rd Ed., Kluwer, The Hague/London/Boston, 1998), explaining the proportionality principle in terms of 'reasonableness,' p. 719, and 'fair balance' p. 723. The 'principle of proportionality' has entered the legal vocabulary in jurisdictions around the world with respect to international, regional and national laws, although sometimes with different terminology. But despite the variations in vocabulary, the reasonableness standard has been said to be the most fundamental norm of state behavior in any field of law; see David M. Beatty, *The Ultimate Rule of Law*.

3.3.1   'States Parties Shall Encourage...'

There are several important things to note about this phrase. In the first place, it does not make sense to speak of a State Party encouraging itself, so all of duties in the second sentence pertain only to the State encouraging others—such as *non-state actors* or *intergovernmental entities*—to do the things laid out in six paragraphs. In the second place, *encourage* is perhaps the least demanding duty in international human rights law. In this context, *encourage* suggests statements of exhortation or inspiration. It would certainly not cover coercive action. And it would be stretching the word to apply it to grants and tax breaks: giving subsidies to private media outlets would be *assisting* or *inducing*, rather than merely *encouraging*. Third, *encourage* gives each State tremendous discretion over the concrete measures it will take, and it does not require the State to ensure any particular result comes from the encouragement. And fourth, the clear inference from the six 'shall encourage...' paragraphs is that the framers did not want to use Article 17 as the vehicle for government regulation of the content of mass media communications.

3.3.2   The Six 'Shall Encourage...' Paragraphs

'[2.]   *To this end,... (a) Encourage the mass media to disseminate information and material of social and cultural benefit to the child and in accordance with the spirit of Article 29*'

There are two things to note. First, the paragraph elaborates slightly on the '[C] *especially those aimed at the promotion of... well-being...*' clause in the first sentence. (That is to say, 'To this end...' is referring to the secondary duty in clause [C].) The elaboration is described as slight because the objects of education in Article 29 are framed in extremely abstract, and lofty, terms, like developing children's talents to the 'fullest potential,' and developing 'respect' for the values of other civilizations. And paragraph (a) makes things more vague by speaking of the 'spirit' of Article 29. This paragraph is a slight elaboration because it adds no concreteness to the secondary duty in the first sentence.

Second, while paragraph (a) only speaks of encouraging the *dissemination* of communications in the spirit of Article 29, there is an implied duty to encourage the production of such material, since it has to be created before it can be disseminated.[34]

---

[34] The opening phrase, 'To this end...,' is a drafting error because 'this end' speaks of one purpose, while each of the three clauses in the first sentence has its own objective. In the 'encour-

'[2.] *To this end, . . . (b) Encourage international co-operation in the production, exchange, and dissemination of such information and material from a diversity of cultural, national, and international sources*'

The language in which this duty is framed is broad enough to cover a number of things. For instance, a State can encourage cooperation between private media sources and research institutes, foundations, and intergovernmental organizations, and it can encourage cooperation with foreign media sources and the private media sources within the country. Moreover, while it makes no sense to speak of a State encouraging itself, it can encourage others to work with the government's media sources. And a State can encourage international cooperation by joining, supporting, and working with international organizations, like UNESCO, and with regional organizations.

'[2.] *To this end, . . . (c) Encourage the production and dissemination of children's books*'

This is the only duty-to-encourage that pertains to a single category of material, and it raises one interpretation question: What does *children's books* refer to? Does it mean any book that is intended to be read by (or read to) people under the age of eighteen years? Probably not.

The Vienna Convention on the Law of Treaties requires that each word be read in accordance with its ordinary meaning, unless a different meaning is clearly indicated. In ordinary speech, *child* refers to a person who has not reached puberty, and it is not applied to young people over the age of fifteen. By contrast, Article 1 says that, 'For the purpose of the present Convention, a child means (i.e., the word 'child' shall be interpreted as meaning) every human being below the age of 18 years unless . . .' So Article 1 creates a legal fiction: it gives an artificial, term-of-art meaning to a word in legal text.[35] Moreover, since the fiction expressly applies to the singular *child*, it does not necessary apply to the plural possessive when used as part of the phrase, *children's book*.

In fact, *children's book* is a set expression that has its own meaning, and it does not include books written for teenagers. Publishers, booksellers, libraries, and

---

age' paragraphs (a) to (e), the end being referred to sometimes shifts from one of these purposes to another.

In the creation of Article 17, the first sentence came from one proposal, and the 'encourage' duties came from another, and the two were spliced together. *Legislative History, o.c.* (note 5), pp. 483–489. But neither the framers, nor the NGOs or intergovernmental organizations at the sessions, nor the people doing the technical reviews, gave thought about how each of the 'encourage' duties in the second sentence related to the two duties and the preamble in the first sentence, so the final text continued to speak in the singular, 'to this end.'

[35] 'The Invisibility of Children and Adolescents,' *o.c.* (note 15), pp. 397–398.

parents divide up books in accordance with age ranges. For instance, from fifteen years upwards, the book industry speaks of 'young adults.' Adolescents have
interests and concerns that are very different from those of children, and the lack
of books written for older teenagers could mean that there is insufficient diversity
of sources in the publishing industry. In addition, many of the books that adolescents read are written for adults; this includes technical books (on computers, for
example), literature, history, philosophy, to name a few. And one should not for-
get that many under-18s are university students, or are enrolled in university level
courses, and have the same thirst for knowledge and love of reading as adults.
'Children's books' does not address the reading needs of older adolescents.

No doubt, the initial reaction of many people is to be gratified to see a duty
to encourage children's books. This product category has been a literary specialty
for authors and publishers for centuries (as least in the West), and not only are
countless adults passionate about reading, most of them probably acquired this
love as children. But upon reflection, it seems arbitrary to have a duty-to-encourage that singles out one just medium (print), and just one product category (children's books). For instance, during the period when the CRC was written, people
throughout the world were demanding better quality in children's programming
in television, and more and better 'family movies.' Viewed in this light, the duty
in paragraph (c) looks arbitrary and exclusive, which suggests that the Working
Group did not have a clear vision of the purpose of Article 17, or gave much
thought to creating the duties-to-encourage so as to coincide with the primary
and secondary duties in the first sentence.[36]

And finally, the traditional meaning of *children's books* does not include books
written *by* children.

'[2.] *To this end, ... (d) Encourage the mass media to have particular regard to the
linguistic needs of the child who belongs to a minority group or who is indigenous'*

The phrase, *to have particular regard to the linguistic needs*, is bureaucratic language. *To have a regard for* something refers to a mental attitude, not to conduct.
Putting it into plain language, the State has a duty to encourage the mass media

---

[36] Paragraph (b) could be read as elaborating on either diversity of sources (in clause [B]), or on
designing materials that will benefit children (in clause [C]), in the first sentence.
  The idea of an encouragement duty pertaining to children's books came from an NGO, the
International Board on Books for Young People, which framed the duty in terms of encouraging
literacy and the reading habit, and which also included encouraging storytelling. *Legislative History,
o.c.* (note 5), p. 489 (paras. 21–23 of the UN. records). This shows the important role of NGOs in
the creation of the CRC. But it also shows the limitations of single-issue lobbyists, and organizations that do not take a holistic, children's rights approach.

'to produce and disseminate material in the languages of' the minority groups and indigenous groups in the State.[37]

This paragraph is a good illustration of how the creation of the Convention reflects the evolution of international affairs. Around the time the CRC was being written, States were much more willing to address the needs of ethnic, linguistic, and indigenous groups in human rights documents, as can be seen in both this paragraph and Article 30, and in other international agreements.[38] But this paragraph also shows the lack of coherence behind Article 17. While the Convention broke ground by devoting a provision entirely to disabled children (Article 23), this Article is silent about encouraging the mass media to design materials for deaf or blind youngsters.[39]

'[2.] *To this end, . . . (e) Encourage the development of appropriate guidelines for the protection of the child from information and material injurious to his or her well-being, bearing in mind the provisions of Articles 13 and 18'*

There are four important things to discuss in this paragraph. First, while the pre-ambular clause recognizes the 'important function' of the mass media, and while the duty to ensure a diversity of sources in the second clause is content-neutral, this paragraph admits there is a dark side: sometimes mass media causes harm to young people.

Second, the duty to encourage the development of guidelines shows that the framers made a political decision: Article 17 is not to be a vehicle for State control of content: Article 17 does not require or authorize State censorship of the content of mass media communications. Nor does it prohibit it. Censorship has to be addressed under other Articles of the CRC, and under other laws (like other UN treaties, regional treaties, and national law).

To put it another way, it is a serious legal mistake to discuss State censorship of mass media content under Article 17. Whether in reporting to the Committee on the Rights of the Child, or in children's rights groups demanding action from the legislature, or in court cases, the authority of a State to protect young people

---

[37] *The child who belongs to a minority group or who is indigenous* is an awkward expression, and it is the result of concerns about political correctness and other sensitivities. For the other language that was considered and discarded, see p. 488 (paras. 68 & 69 of the UN records) and p. 492 (para. 322 of the UN records). The same language appears in Article 30.

[38] E.g., in 1989, the International Labour Organization adopted Convention (No. 169) Concerning Indigenous and Tribal Peoples in Independent Countries; in 1992, the UN General Assembly adopted the Declaration on the Rights of Persons Belonging to National or Ethnic, Religious and Linguistic Minorities; and in 1995, the Council of Europe adopted the Framework Convention for the Protection of National Minorities (see especially Articles 9 and 10).

[39] In the phrase, '*To this end, . . . ,*' it is not clear which end paragraph (d) is referring to.

from harmful content, and the limitations to State control, must be handled under other articles of the CRC, and other legal sources.

Third, there is no explicit statement of who is to develop guidelines for protecting young people from harmful communications. This silence is often remarked upon, but sometimes people jump to the conclusion that the duty can be discharged by the State creating the guidelines. Since it does not make sense to talk of a State encouraging itself, the framers must have had in mind the State encouraging others to do it, such as the privately owned industries, or independent bodies set up by the State, or States collectively on a regional basis.[40]

And finally, the *bearing in mind the provisions of Articles 13 and 18* clause needs to be examined. As discussed earlier, Article 13 contains a provision that allows (and perhaps even requires) a State to limit a right-holder's entitlement to receive a communication for the sake of morality, public order, and the rights of others. So 'bearing in mind...Article 13' is a direct recognition that the State can censor private mass media, albeit not under Article 17.

'Bearing in mind...Article 18' is more complicated. Article 18 says, among other things, that parents have *the primary* responsibility for the well-being of their children, and that, despite what the other articles say, the State only has the duty 'to take *appropriate measures to assist* the parents' (emphasis added), with the State deciding what is 'appropriate.' The implication for Article 17 seems to be that the parents have to control what mass media communicates to their children, even though, as a practical matter, they have little or no power to do this, while the State, which has enormous power, plays a backseat role.

Now the significance of 'bearing in mind...' is apparent. This language deliberately avoids clarifying the State's role in relation to the parents' role in protecting young people from harmful material sent by the mass media. During the negotiations over Article 17, some States wanted to explicitly put the burden on parents, while other States wanted to make sure that the Article did not address State censorship in any way.[41] In the end, the framers of Article 17 evaded the question of how to allocate responsibility for regulating the amount and kinds of harm that mass media sources are allowed to inflict on children in the pursuit of profits and other agendas. 'Bearing in mind' is vague language that dodges the critical problem of State responsibility to protect children from harmful mass media material.[42]

---

[40] In the phrase, '*To this end,...*,' it is doubtful that paragraph (e) actually refers to any of the three purposes in the first sentence. If that is so, then this is another drafting error.

[41] See the discussion of the legislative history in section 3.7.

[42] In the phrase, 'development of appropriate guidelines,' *appropriate* is superfluous, and could have been eliminated without affecting the State's duty. See, e.g., Department of Conference

3.3.3   *'To This End, States Parties Shall…'*

'To this end, States Parties shall…' can be read in two ways: (i) Paragraphs (a) to (e) are an *exhaustive list* of what a State must do to fulfill Article 17. That is to say, the second sentence restricts the primary and secondary duties in the first sentence to only the actions in those six paragraphs. Or, (ii) the second sentence *identifies only some of things* that the State must do.

The list is clearly not exhaustive. First, the 'shall ensure…' duties cannot be realized just by acts of *encouragement*. Second, the duties cannot be fulfilled only by encouragement directed at private media sources, since most all States are producers and disseminators of mass media communication. And third, the exhaustive-reading would reduce the duties in the '[C] especially those aimed at the promotion of…well-being…' clause to just children's books (in paragraph (b)), leaving out other media industries, and other types of books. So the second sentence merely specifies some of the things that the State needs to do to fulfill its primary and secondary duties in the first sentence.

There are several important consequences to this interpretation. For one, a State is not prevented from taking coercive measures to achieve the beneficial end-results referred to in the six paragraphs, if the regulatory measures are reasonable steps to fulfill the 'shall ensure…' duties in the first sentence, or to fulfill some other legal duty (as in the case of protecting youngsters from sexual exploitation, for instance). For another, depending on the circumstances, the 'shall ensure…' duties could require a State to do some of the things that the private media sources are only encouraged to do. For instance, complying with the first sentence could require a State to engage in international cooperation, or to establish guidelines to protect minors from harmful content disseminated by State-owned media sources, or to order the State's book publishing department to increase production of children's books, and to publish in the languages of the nation's ethnic groups.

3.3.4   *Implied Duties*

In law in general, the duties that are expressly stated usually give rise to implied duties: by logic and practical necessity, one derives implied duties from the explicated stated duties. In court cases, for example, implied duties are 'read into' the text by judges.

The 'shall ensure…' duties in Article 17 give rise to a number of implied duties. These include:

Services, *A Guide to Writing for the United Nations* (United Nations, New York, 1984), UN Doc. ST/DCS/3, p. 28 (identifying *appropriate* as one of the 'deadhead' words of bad writing).

- a duty to limit the concentration of private ownership of mass media, whenever such limitations are necessary to ensure a reasonable amount of diversity of production and dissemination sources;
- a duty to make sure that all restrictions on private ownership and management of mass media sources are reasonable (i.e., a duty to not impose unreasonable restrictions); and
- a duty to make sure that only reasonable restrictions are put on the dissemination of mass media communications coming from outside the country.

There are also implied duties pertaining to the progressive fulfillment of Article 17's obligations. These include:

- a duty to have a reasonable amount of statistical information on the availability of media sources to young people overall, and to various segments of the population (e.g., the percentage of young people with Internet in their homes, and schools; the percentage of young people in rural areas with television in their homes);
- a duty to have reasonable amounts of statistical information and studies on the various barriers to access to mass media sources;
- a duty to have a multi-year plan to increase availability, a duty to make reasonable progress in carrying out the plan, a duty to monitor and evaluate the progress, and a duty to be transparent about the plan, the progress, and the monitoring (i.e., disclose them to the public);
- a duty to adopt laws, policies, and programs that will increase the availability of a diversity of mass media sources, whenever young people overall or certain segments of young people lack access (e.g., young people who live in rural areas, or have hearing or vision impairments); 'diversity' must be defined in multiple ways, including by mediums of communication (e.g., Internet, radio, TV, books, magazines), and by types of materials (e.g., children's books, books for young adults);
- a duty to give priority to the most severely underserved segments of the population (e.g., significant budget allocations to increase availability to children in remote areas, or to children with communication disabilities, or to build infrastructures for satellite communications and the Internet); and
- a duty to engage in cooperation with international actors, and with civil society actors within the country, whenever the State lacks the resources to ensure a reasonable level of access to a diversity of sources, especially to sources that produce or disseminate materials designed to be beneficial to children and adolescents.

None of these duties are explicitly stated in Article 17; but all of them are logically derived from the primary and secondary duties in the first sentence.

Identifying implied duties is not an academic exercise. Implied duties (and implied rights) are crucial for legislative and administrative action, for lobbying and campaigning, and for litigation. Generally speaking, implied duties (and implied rights) are the single most powerful legal tool for courts to turn words in a legal text into State action that benefits people.

3.3.5   Is Article 17 an Individually Held Right or a 'Group Right'?

Most of the provisions in Part I of the CRC (i.e., Articles 1 to 41) are rights that are held by each child or adolescent on an individual basis. For instance, 'States Parties recognize that every child has the inherent right to life' (Article 6(1)) is obviously a personally held right. But some are not individually held rights. The duty to 'undertake all appropriate legislative, administrative, and other measures for the implementation of the rights recognized in the present Convention' (Article 4) is a duty to take action in respect to children in a collective, or *en masse*, manner; fulfillment of this duty does not call for the State to individualize the action for each CRC right-holder personally.[43]

Likewise, the duty to ensure the availability of a reasonable amount of diversity in mass media sources is a duty to take action that will impact young people in collective, *en masse* ways. In discharging its duties, a State will take a variety of measures, and in designing these measures it may often think in terms of categories or demographic groups of children and adolescents; but it will not think in terms of each child individually. While the idea of 'group rights' is controversial as a legal concept (who is the right-holder who decides how to exercise the right? for instance), calling Article 17 a 'group right' is still the best way to describe it using the language of rights.

It might be argued that Article 17 creates personally held rights, citing as evidence the text itself; for instance: the State shall 'encourage the mass media to disseminate' material that is beneficial 'to the child' (paragraph (a)). But throughout Article 17 *the child* is a collective noun, and it means the plural *children*, in the sense of children generally, as a large scale demographic group. That is way the framers did not write, 'Every child shall have the right to access to...' but framed the obligation only as a duty: 'States Parties...shall ensure that the child [children] have access to...'

---

[43] Other examples: Article 1 is the 'jurisdictional clause' that, along with the 'within their jurisdiction' clause in Article 2(1), defines the class of persons who are covered by the treaty. Article 3(1) is a procedural rule that applies to state decision-making that concerns (i.e., is about) children in a collective, *en masse* way. And while Article 5 gives rights, it gives them to the parents.

3.3.6   *Summary of the Legal Interpretation*

According to Thomas Hammarberg, a prominent children's right spokesman, and a member of the Committee when it came into being in the early 1990s, 'One problem is that the Convention is used in an ignorant manner. Not seldom are its provisions overstated,...'[44] That is strong criticism. Is Mr. Hammarberg exaggerating the problem?

Here are some representative examples of how Article 17 is being presented to young people, the public at large, and in the academic literature. One publication explains: 'Children have the right to reliable information from the mass media.'[45] Another tells young people: 'You have the right of information. You have the right to receive information that is diversified and objective.'[46] Another simplifies the Article as: 'You have a right to get information from lots of different places.'[47] Another says: 'Through the media you have a right to obtain information that will benefit you.'[48] A distinguished author describes it as 'the right to access to the media.'[49] And another publication condenses it to 'Access to information.'[50]

Every one of those paraphrases and simplifications distorts Article 17 beyond recognition. None of them takes the CRC seriously as international law, reading the text carefully, and interpreting it in accordance with the rules of treaty interpretation. At least those are the conclusions to be drawn when judged in the light of the legal analysis in this chapter.[51]

---

[44] Thomas Hammarberg, 'Children, the UN Convention and the Media,' *International Journal of Children's Rights*, Vol. 5, 1997, p. 245.

[45] UNICEF, *What Rights? Summary of the Convention on the Rights of the Child* (flyer, not dated), available at www.unicef.org/magic/briefing/uncorc-html. It goes on to say: 'Television, radio, and newspapers should provide information that children can understand, and should not promote materials that could harm children.'

[46] 'Convention on the Rights of the Child,' *YMCA World* (World Alliance of YMCAs), Dec., 2001, p. 111. Moreover, readers are not told that the Articles are paraphrases.

[47] The Children's Law Centre, *Do You Know Your Rights?* (Children's Law Centre & CHALKY Freephone Helpline, Belfast, no date [circa 2005]). It continues: 'The information should be given in a way that you can understand. Information that may be harmful to you should not be easy to get.'

[48] 'What's Up CROC?' (web page), available at www.ncylc.org.au/croc/what.html.

[49] 'Children, the UN Convention and the media,' *o.c.* (note 44), p. 251.

[50] 'United Nations' Convention on the Rights of the Child (Summary),' *Echoes*, vol. 20, 2001, p. 39. It continues, starting with an incomplete sentence: 'The role of the media in disseminating information to children that is consistent with moral well-being and knowledge and understanding among peoples, and respects the child's cultural background. The state is to take measures to encourage this and to protect children from harmful materials.'

[51] One well done paraphrase: 'Governments have the responsibility to make sure that information and material is available to us from many sources, both national and international, especially when it is aimed at promoting our well-being and health.' Youth Participation Committee, Canadian Coalition for the Rights of Children, 'Say It Right! The Canadian Youth Edition of the Unconventional United Nations Convention on the Rights of the Child' (Canadian Resource

To summarize the interpretation. Under the first sentence of Article 17, the primary duty pertains to *access to a diversity of sources*: the State must ensure the availability of a variety of mass media sources. The secondary duty pertains to a type of *content*: the State must make sure that, among this diversity of sources, there are producers and disseminators of materials aimed at promoting the well-being of young people. The text does not contain the standard of duty, so an implied element must be read into the Article: there must be a *reasonable amount* of variety, and, within this variety, there must be a *reasonable number* of sources that produce and disseminate beneficial materials. And finally, the first sentence does not address the need for restrictions on harmful media content; it neither requires, or authorizes State censorship.

In the second sentence, all of the State's duties pertain to encouraging non-state and intergovernmental actors to do things that relate, in various ways, to the primary or secondary duties in the first sentence. And, since paragraph (e) only requires the State to encourage other actors to create guidelines for protecting against harmful content, it is a legal error to discuss State censorship under Article 17.

One of the most powerful legal tools for making the promises in Article 17 a reality is to particularize the abstract, expressed duties into more concrete, implied duties.

Finally, Article 17 can be described as a 'group (or collective) right,' in contrast to freedom of expression other human rights that are held on an individual basis.

3.3.7   *Legislative History*

People use the legislative history of the CRC primarily out of historical interest, and only secondarily for legal interpretation. One reason why the records play a minor role in legal interpretation is because they usually contain little or no information that is useful in resolving important legal questions about the Convention. Another reason is because the records play a subordinate role under the rules of interpretation in the Vienna Convention on the Law of Treaties.

The primary rule of treaty interpretation, the 'ordinary meaning rule,' does not permit the records to be used in the analysis. The rule deals with the text of the treaty, and with what logic and common sense derives for the words of the text, when read in context, including the objectives of the treaty. Only when the

---

Centre on Children and Youth (a program of the Child Welfare League of Canada), Ottawa, Ontario no date), p. 8.

ordinary meaning rule produces an interpretation that is 'manifestly absurd' can the records be used to interpret a provision.

When an interpretation passes the 'manifestly absurd' test, the legislative history can be used to *confirm* the reading; that is to say, the records can be used to give satisfaction with the reasoning in the application of the ordinary meaning rule and with the interpretation that it produced, which also might help persuade doubters to accept or at least acquiesce in the interpretation. But the legislative history cannot be used to replace or change the interpretation arrived at by the ordinary meaning rule: the text, and what human reasoning can derive from the text, is definitive. Only when the interpretation is manifestly absurd can the records of the negotiations and drafting be used to *produce an interpretation*.[52]

> therefore, the assumption is that there will be general agreement that the interpretations in this chapter do not fail the 'manifestly absurd' test. Therefore a review of the legislative history to see if it confirms the interpretations, and for whatever insights it can provide about the history and politics of the creation of the Convention.

Confirmation of the Interpretation

Nothing was found in the records that contradicts the interpretation; but also, what is there only confirms the interpretations in a general way. That is to say, it describes what the framers intended to put into the Article is indeed what the text says; there were not any breakdowns in the writing of the text that caused it to say something different from what the framers had agreed. But there are no clear statements that directly speak to important questions. For instance, it was argued that the focus of the primary duty is on ensuring access to a diversity of sources, rather than on access to communications that, only incidentally, come from a diversity of sources. There is nothing in the records that directly settles this. There are a few passages that show clear intentions of various delegates, such as: 'the mass media does far more good than harm and therefore the article should

---

[52] The ordinary meaning rule, Article 3(1) of the VCLT, is quoted in full in sec. 3.1. Article 32 reads:

> Recourse may be had to supplementary means of interpretation, including the preparatory work of the treaty and the circumstances of its conclusion, in order
> [1] to *confirm* the meaning resulting from the application of Article 31, or
> [2] to *determine* the meaning when the interpretation according to Article 31:
>> (a) leaves the meaning ambiguous or obscure; or
>> (b) leads to a result which is manifestly absurd or unreasonable. (Brackets and emphasis added.)
>
> Article 32[1] is the corollary to the ordinary meaning rule in Article 31(1), and it allows the records to be used for confirmation of the interpretation produced by that rule; but the records cannot be used to replace or alter that interpretation. Article 32[2] is the 'legislative history rule,' the fallback rule that is used for producing an interpretation when the ordinary meaning rule fails.

be phrased in positive terms, rather than in terms of seeking to protect children from the mass media;' that it is important to guarantee children 'access to information from a diversity of sources;' the article should aim to allow children 'to take advantage of a diversity of opinion concerning all matters;'[53] 'the dangers of censorship' need to be considered when evaluating the original working draft;[54] and 'the whole thrust of (the article in its almost final version) was aimed rather at the spread of information than its limitation.'[55] But all of these intentions can be found either in the text itself or easily deduced from it, and do not directly settle any important interpretation question.[56]

Insights into History and Politics
Despite the lack of usefulness of the records in interpreting the Article 17, a review of the evolution of the negotiations over the text provides some valuable insights.

The original working draft looked at mass media in a negative light, and called for protective measures: '*Parents*, guardians, *State organs* and social organizations *shall protect* the child against *any* harmful influences that mass media...*may* exert...' (emphasis added).[57] This led to a proposal championed by the Soviet Union that, among other things, said 'States Parties shall *encourage parents* to provide their children with appropriate *guidance*...' (emphasis added).[58] There were numerous cries of protest against these negative approaches, most of which were quoted above. The next important development came a year later with two counterproposals. An NGO suggested a text that contained a string of duties to 'encourage,' which, after being adopted, evolved into the second sentence of Article 17.[59] At the same time, the United States proposed a text that, with a few changes, became the first sentence of the Article.[60]

One of the most significant differences between the U.S. text and the final version of the first sentence is that the proposal contained a provocative phrase: 'ensure that the child has access to information from a diversity of sources, *in particular by not impeding the free flow of information across international borders*...' (emphasis added). The United States was playing Cold War politics with the Soviet Union, just as the two of them had done in the negotiations over

---

[53] All three quotations from *Legislative History, o.c.* (note 5), p. 481 (paras. 120 and 121 of the UN records).
[54] Ibid., p. 483 (para. 38 of the UN records).
[55] Ibid., p. 492 (para. 325 of the UN records).
[56] For the part of the records that come the closest to being an exception to this generalization.
[57] Ibid., p. 480 (Revised Polish draft (1979), sec. C.1 of the History).
[58] Ibid., pp. 482–483 (para. 36 of the UN records).
[59] Ibid., p. 483 (suggestion of Baha'i International Community, sec. 7(b) of the History).
[60] Ibid., p. 485 (para. 53 of the UN records).

the Universal Declaration and the two Covenants. The expression *free flow* once again pits the 'Free West' against the 'Iron Curtain.' Moreover, from its inception the Soviet Union had been suppressing the press, and all other avenues of expression, within its borders and in the States it controlled. This included the Soviet's jamming of the U.S.'s Radio Free Europe broadcasts into its territories, in a cat-and-mouse game where the network kept changing the frequencies to elude the jamming just long enough to reach an audience that was eagerly keeping on top of the game. This contest is reflected in the U.S. proposal: *in particular, the free flow of information across international boarders.*

The Soviet Union predictably rose to the provocation, and the United States quickly agreed to substitute the offending words with language that still imposes a duty to ensure access to international sources, but without the Cold War wording.[61] It was a clever maneuver, by making a little compromise, the United States got an agreement to add an obligation that not only is unique in international law, but that also has a powerful potential to change the quality of the everyday lives of people, and the democratic quality of the political processes—the duty to ensure that people have access to a diversity of mass media sources.

The NGO suggestion and the U.S. proposal were immediately spliced together and soon adopted,[62] and the remaining years of the negotiations were spent in adding some other 'encouragement' duties, and polishing the language.

This brief outline of the history leads to some sociological and political reflections. For one, the U.S. proposal is a clear echo of the MacBride Report: '[A]n essential criterion of freedom of information is [A] diversity of sources, coupled with [B] free access to these sources' (brackets added). Those two ideas are captured exactly in the U.S. proposal.[63]

In [B], 'free access' to these sources is political rhetoric that means the second side of freedom of expression—the right to receive communications—with *free* being a euphemism for 'reasonable,' freedom from *unreasonable* state-regulation of communications. But before the public can receive communications, the sources of production and dissemination must exist, and, as [A] makes clear, freedom of information demands 'a diversity of sources.' The MacBride quote continues:

---

[61] Ibid., pp. 486–487 (especially paras. 55, and 63–65 of the UN records). The USSR acted through the Ukrainian SSR; although it was a political subdivision of the USSR, it had been granted admission as a Member of the United Nations in a Cold War compromise.

[62] Ibid., pp. 485–489 (paras. 54 & 56 [adopting it as the basis for discussion], and para. 79 [adopting it as the new text], of the UN records).

[63] MacBride Report, *o.c.* (note 6), p. 22.

A concentration of such sources under the control of dominant groups, tends, whatever the political system, to make a mockery of freedom. A wide spectrum of information and opinion is necessary to equip the citizen to make well-founded judgments on political issues, and is thus a vital ingredient of any communication system in a democratic society, and *access to a diversity of sources* is as desirable on an international as on a national level. (Emphasis added.)

Diversity in sources must exist. The sources create and disseminate communications, and people have a right to receive those messages. But first the sources must exist, and they must exist in variety if the needs of a democratic society are to be met.

During the legal interpretation, it was debated where the emphasis should go in the phrase, *access to information and material from a diversity of national and international sources.* It was argued that the focus should be on ensuring 'access to a diversity of sources.' That is the focus in the MacBride Report, and that is the viewpoint in the U.S. proposal.

All of Article 17 exists as a result of an adverse reaction to the negative approaches to the mass media taken by the original proposals. The Article did not arise from pre-existing concerns about the relation between children and the mass media. This probably is what explains the arbitrariness in the content of the Article, and why its falls short of the standards of legal craftsmanship found in other provisions in the CRC and the other UN human rights treaties. For example, the Articles on education, health, and juvenile justice have behind them long histories of UN agencies, academic specialists, foundations, and NGOs defining the problems, developing solutions, and shaping public understandings and opinions. And this professionalism, and the participations of these interests groups at the Working Group, is seen in the coherence, completeness, and craftsmanship of those Articles. By contrast, Article 17 was an ad hoc endeavor, born of adverse reactions to the original proposals and of Cold War politics.

Article 17 is still in the process of overcoming the disadvantages of the circumstances of its birth. The marginalization of Article 17 will be examined in the next chapter on the implementation of the Article.

Neither the review of the legislative history, nor any of these socio-political reflections, has any bearing on producing the legal interpretation. The meaning of the Article is determined by the text of the CRC, as read in accordance with the ordinary meaning rule of the VCLT.

CHAPTER FOUR

IMPLEMENTATION OF ARTICLE 17 AS SEEN THROUGH THE PERSPECTIVES OF THE COMMITTEE

4.1. *Implementation As Seen through the Days of Discussion*

Day of Discussion: The Child and the Media (1996)

The Committee on the Rights not only monitors the States Parties' fulfillments of their duties, but also to 'enhance a deeper understanding of the content and implications of the Convention.'[64] Its two main tools are the General Comments and the Days of Discussions on Important topics. In 1996, the Committee held a Day of Discussion on 'The Child and the Media.' In the preliminary documents prepared for the Discussion, it was stated that:

> The Committee on the Rights of the Child believes that the media—both written and audiovisual—are highly important in the efforts to make reality the principles and standards of the Convention. The media in many countries have already contributed greatly in creating an awareness of the Convention and its content. The media could also play a pivotal role in monitoring the actual implementation of the rights of the child.[65]

The media is also referred to a contributory agent to the harm of children:

> Concern has also been expressed about the influence on children of negative aspects of the media, primarily programmes containing brutal violence and pornography. There is discussion in a number of countries about how to protect children from violence on television in video films and in other modern media. Again, voluntary agreements have been attempted, with varied impact. This particular problem is raised in Article 17 of the Convention, which recommends that appropriate guidelines be developed 'for the protection of the child from information and material injurious to his or her well-being.'[66]

The Day of Discussion was divided into three topics:

> *'Child participation in the media'* centered around the importance of children participating not just as commentators, but at all levels of the information process.[67]

---

[64] Excerpted from CRC/C/50, Annex IX, 13th Session, 7 October 1996.
[65] Ibid., p. 1.
[66] Ibid.
[67] Ibid., p. 4.

'Protection of the child against harmful influences through the media' determined there
was a need to keep children on the media's agenda on a continuing basis and that
States should be called upon to take concrete measures to encourage the mass media
to disseminate information and material of social and cultural benefit to the child
and in accordance with the spirit of Article 29 of the Convention, as called for in
Article 17(a).[68]

'Respect for the integrity of the child in media reporting' recognized that the media
played an essential role in the promotion and protection of human rights in general
and that media professionals, including media editors and owners, should be particularly vigilant in trying to safeguard the integrity of the child.[69]

The participants agreed that the media is a vital player in society, and that it
directly affects the perceptions and behaviors of people. The outcome document
underscored the need for clearer definitions of media, and for better pinpointing
of who has responsibility to monitor the media. The Committee ended up making
twelve recommendations. These included the creation of guidelines for journalists who interview children or write about them, encouraging media producers to
include the views of children in their programs, the promotion of 'child-friendly
media' (e.g., on Internet sites, in the mainstream press and in libraries), providing
children with training in media literacy, encouraging States to sponsor the development of children's media (including the arts), and equipping electronic devices
with blocking functions so that parents can better safeguard their children from
harmful or unsuitable material.[70]

The Day of Discussion was the Committee's first foray into the diverse nature
of the media, the child's right to freedom of expression in regard to the media,
children's access to the media, and the State's role in assuring that a variety of
ideas and information will be available to children. However, by restricting the
discussion to topics like content and freedom of expression, no attention was
paid to the State's obligations under Article 17—to ensure that children have
access to a diversity of mass media sources.

Day of Discussion: The Child's Right to be Heard (2006)

Ten years later, the Committee chose the Child's Right to be Heard as the
theme of its Day of Discussion in 2006. This time, steps were taken so children
participated both in person and in writing. The main topics were Articles 12 and
13, which were discussed in two groups: Allowing the child's views to be heard

---

[68] Ibid., pp. 4–5.
[69] Ibid., p. 5.
[70] Ibid., p. 7.

in judicial settings, and the broader subject of participation—in school, public forums, youth organizations and so forth.

One of the papers submitted to the Discussion did a legal analysis of Article 12, and it argued that the right to be listened to only applies to state-actors making decisions about individual children, or about a group of children that is small enough for the actor to listen to each one of them. Among other things, the paper considered the very high standard of the duty: the State 'shall assure to the child...' Since the State cannot police private life to the degree required to meet such a standard, one must conclude that the framers did not intend for the Article to apply to the decision-making of non-state actors:

> The State can make promises about its own behavior, but not about the behavior of private persons over whom it does not have direct control. The State could promise that it will take steps aimed at ensuring non-state actors will do such-and-such, but it would be foolish to make a legally binding commitment to assure the conduct of people that it does not have the right or the power to supervise and control.[71]

If that interpretation is correct, then the State does not have to assure that every decision made by every person working in the mass media listens to, and takes into account, the views of every child who could be affected by that decision. Article 12 would not be a vehicle for a State to regulate the way that journalists, musicians, business managers, and so forth go about making and disseminating mass media materials in the private sector.

4.2. Implementation As Seen through the State Reports

States usually follow the Committee's Guidelines for reporting, and they look at how other States are writing their reports. If the guideline for an Article is not clear, specific and complete, then States would probably not give the information that is needed for good monitoring of children from harmful content, which does not come under the scope of Article 17.

The implementation reports give very little information about what is being done to fulfill Article 17. The main reason for this failure is the Committee's Guidelines. The initial and the periodic Guidelines ask no questions about ensuring diversity of mass media sources.

The Guidelines place Article 17, together with Article 13 (freedom of expression), under the thematic heading or cluster of 'Civil and Political Rights.' This ignores the fact that the duty to ensure a diversity of mass media sources

---

[71] Abramson, Bruce. 'Does Article 12 Apply to State Actors Only, Or Does It Include All Private Actors?,' Individual submission, 30 August 2006, "The Child's Right to be Heard."

impacts the social-cultural-and-economic aspects of life, and it leads to confusions between the negative liberty right of freedom of expression and the positive obligations to ensure that adolescents and children have a diversity of mass media sources to choose from.

Moreover, the Guidelines ask just one question, and the question is about content: 'States Parties should provide relevant information in respect of:...(g) Access to appropriate information (Art. 17)...' The word 'appropriate' leads people to think that the Committee wants, among other things, information about protecting children from harmful content, which is a matter for Article 13 and other provisions, and not something to be reported on under Article 17. And the word 'relevant' does not give any guidance to the States.[72]

Thomas Hammarberg, who was a member of the Committee from 1991 to 1997, published an article that provided insight into the Committee's views of the obligations under Article 17. However, he spoke of *content of information* interchangeably with *diversity of sources* of that information. He also said, 'It is not clear from the wording whose responsibility it is to develop guidelines, only that the State should be encouraging [the media industries to have them]....the vagueness of the Convention in this regard can be seen as an invitation to a discussion on objectives rather than an offering of precise methods of implementation. The very nature of the guidelines is also unclear, except for the their purpose to protect children.'[73]

In a survey of the reports of fifty States,[74] two scenarios emerge with regard to the reporting on Article 17: 1) little or nothing is mentioned; or 2) they say that the 'right to free expression' is guaranteed in their Constitution, or that laws protecting children from harmful influences have been incorporated into domestic jurisprudence, and thus Article 17 is fulfilled. Moreover, what is reported on was often not followed by recommendations in the Committees' Concluding Observations, and Article 17 was sometimes not referenced at all. Hammarberg

---

[72] The quotation is from CRC Comm., 'General Guidelines Regarding the Form and Content of Periodic Reports [ ],' UN Doc. CRC/C/58/rev.1 (2005), para. 25. The one concrete request is for 'statistics on the number of libraries accessible to children, including mobile libraries.' Ibid., Annex, para. 9. The 'General Guidelines Regarding the Form and Content of Initial Reports [ ]' is identical, except it has no annex; Doc. CRC/C/5 (1991), para. 15(d). The original guidelines for periodic reports, used from 1996 to 2005, demanded an oppressive amount of information on most articles. But despite the thoroughness, the wording of the guideline for Article 17 did not make it clear that the focus of the primary duty in on ensuring diversity of sources. 'General Guidelines Regarding the Form and Content of Periodic Reports [ ],' UN Doc. CRC/C/58 (1996), para. 60.

[73] Hammarberg, Thomas, International Journal of Children's Rights, *Children, the UN Convention and the Media*, Volume 5, page 255.

[74] The fifty States included representation from all regions of the world, and included both large and small States. Notably, in order to have information to report, many countries had no reference to Article 17, thus limiting the available research.

saw the inconsistencies in another way: 'Two tendencies emerge from the country reports: 1) that fairly little is done to make it possible for children to participate actively in the media and 2) that economic restraints in a number of countries also hinder children from media consumption.'[75]

Based on the legal analysis in Chapter Three, a number of core questions are identified that the Guidelines should be asking, but are not. This section will compare what States are saying in their reports to these essential questions.

The primary duty, which is in the first sentence of Article 17, is to ensure diversity in the availability of mass media sources. There are six core questions regarding this duty.

(1) Diversity of Ownership.

   (a) *The report should state the number of radio stations, television stations, and newspapers in the country, and then describe*:
   (b) *the extent of State ownership, and*
   (c) *the extent of the concentration of private ownership, in each medium.*

According to the CRC literature, concentration of ownership is a current problem, at least in some countries. For example, Brazilian researcher Dênis de Moraes, from the Federal University of Rio de Janeiro (UFRJ), stated that the excessive predominance of media and entertainment oligopolies in the region was triggered by deregulation and the deliberate neglect of the three branches of government in discharging their regulatory and oversight duties.[76] He explained that, 'An obstacle to more vigorous public debate on communications in the region involves the concentration of media ownership and its impact on the diversity of imparted information. Examples of this tendency are the large media production/exporting conglomerates in Latin America—including Brazil, (Rede Globo), Mexico (Televisa) and Venezuela (Cisneros).'[77]

From a global vantage point, media author Ben Bagdikan observed, 'There may be a large number of outlets giving the appearance of diversity, but a concern is that so many are owned by one of the few media giants. Unfortunately, the large numbers deepen the problem of excessively concentrated control. If the

---

[75] T. Hammarberg, *o.c.* (note 73), page 252.
[76] Rights, Childhood, and Public Agenda: A comparative analysis of Latin American press coverage/News Agency for Children's Rights; ANDI Latin America Network.—Brasilia: ANDI, 2007, p. 7.
[77] Ibid., p. 17.

number of outlets is growing and the number of owners declining, then each owner controls even more formidable communications power.'[78]

Ecuador's report provided a good example of concrete information about numbers:

> Ecuador has 1,184 short-wave, AM and FM radio stations and relay stations; 331 broadcast TV stations (VHF and UHF); 195 cable television stations; and 26 daily newspapers with nationwide, regional and/or provincial coverage that are members of the Ecuadorian Association of Newspaper Publishers (AEDEP). However, there are a variety of local newspapers in different localities of the country that do not belong to this association and there is no accurate record of their number because no government agency monitors and records the work of Ecuadorian newspapers. According to the National Radio and Television Council (CONARTEL), most existing stations, especially television stations, are commercial.'[79]

But notice that the last sentence does not give any concrete information about diversity of ownership, since 'most stations are commercial' could mean anything from 51% to 99%, and it says nothing about concentration of ownership. For example, if two businesses own most of the private stations, and the State owns nearly half of the total, then there is over concentration in both the private and the public sectors.

(2) Diversity of Origins of Production. *The report should State the approximate percentage of materials that come from national, regional, and other international sources for radio, television, movies, CDs, and books.*

No State gave information on this subject, although several reported on their efforts to increase the production of materials within the country (which is discussed below).

(3) Restrictions on Sources. *The report should describe any laws and policies that restrict diversity of sources. This includes:*

(a) *restrictions on private ownership of newspapers, and of radio and television production and dissemination sources, including ownership by foreign persons or corporations;*

(b) *restrictions on dissemination of materials that are produced by foreign sources; and*

(c) *restrictions on access to the Internet.*

---

[78] Ben H. Bagdikian, The Media Monopoly, Sixth Edition, (Beacon Press, 2000), p. 222 (Emphasis Added).

[79] CRC/C/ECU/4, p. 48, para. 184.

There is no reference to these matters in the Reports surveyed, although from other sources it appears that a number of States are restricting foreign content via the mass media, particularly the Internet.

For example, in Kyrgyzstan in 2010, protests broke out when the government began revoking the licenses of radio operators.

> Critics of President Kurmanbek S. Bakiyev said the government was trying to silence Radio Free Europe/Radio Liberty's Kyrgyz service, know locally as Radio Azattyk, as part of an attempt to stifle independent reporting. Since coming to power in 2005, Mr. Bakkiyez has tightened his grip over the impoverished former Soviet satellite, promoting fears of deepening authoritarianism. Radio Azattyk has been unavailable across most of Kyrgyzstan since last Wednesday after several of the station's local partners revoked their broadcasting deals.[80]

And in March 2010, Google, the Internet search engine giant, criticized China's jamming of Google citing 'significant and serious economic implications' and 'human rights issues.'[81]

(4) Increasing Diversity. *The report should say what the State is doing to increase the variety in sources with respect to*:

(a) *diversity of ownership, and*
(b) *diversity of origins of production and dissemination (i.e., national, regional, and outside the region).*

No State in the survey reported on efforts to increase diversity in ownership. As for diversity in origin, several States said they were taking steps to increase the production of materials within the country. For example: Uganda said that 'the government has made an effort to increase the availability of and access to information materials for children for academic instruction, general information and entertainment.' However, the details were quite limited: 'The Government has approved the use of materials produced and published locally for the school curriculum; these are more relevant, cheaper and accessible to more people than the traditionally used books that were imported from outside the country.'[82] *Trinidad and Tobago* reported: 'The Government Information Services Division produces programmes of national interest including programmes which target the youth.'[83] And *Canada* said that 'Financial assistance for the production of Canadian

---

[80] International Herald Tribune, 16 March 2010, p. 15 'Kyrgyz rally to support US-backed radio service' Associated Press.
[81] MarketWatch, "Google executive calls for censorship trade rules", 24 March 2010.
[82] CRC/C/65/Add.33, p. 35.
[83] CRC/C/83/Add.12, p. 168.

children's programming is provided by both the private sector and the Canadian government.'[84] Unfortunately, this information is too sparse to allow for an evaluation of the degree of fulfillment of the State's obligations.

Looking for information from outside of the State Reports, it appears measures are being taken to increase diversity. For instance, in 2010, the British Broadcasting Company (BBC) began to reorganize the State-subsidized media empire, resulting in much speculation as to whether it would be good or bad for the British people. Mark Thompson, the Director-General of the BBC, admitted that the corporation, which is funded by £3.6 billion in annual license fees, has become too large and must shrink to give its commercial rivals room to operate.[85]

Increasing the availability of the Internet and satellite transmissions is especially important because that will greatly expand the amount of foreign-produced and -disseminated communications (see below).

(5) Access to Mass Media

   (a) *The report should describe the availability of sources in ratios of source-to-population for the key mediums of mass communication. This includes: newspapers, radio stations, television stations, libraries, homes with connections to satellite television and to the Internet, and the availability to children of the Internet in other situations (e.g., schools, libraries, and Internet cafes).*
   (b) *The report should describe geographical disparities in availability.*

Some States in the survey report that there is poor availability of distribution outlets, but no State gave statistical information. For instance, *Timor-Leste* said 'the obstacles facing [its] nationwide mass media have meant that a large proportion of children have very limited access to reliable mass media and other information sources.' But without data on the ratios of source-to-population, there is no way to evaluate the situation, or assess progress.

Moreover, no State in the survey gave specific information on geographical disparities in the availability of mass media sources, although several said that rural areas have less access to mass-distributed content than more populated areas.

(6) Increasing Availability and Ease of Utilization. *The report should describe the State's laws, policies, and programs aimed at*:

---

[84] Ibid., para. 106.
[85] The Times, *BBC Signals End to Era of Expansion*, 26 February 2010.

(a) *Increasing the availability (i.e., existence) of a diversity of mass media sources. This includes making new mediums available (e.g., the Internet), and reducing regional disparities in distribution sources.*

(b) *Increasing the ease of utilization of sources by reducing economic and other barriers.*[86]

While some reports lament the lack of distribution sources, they do not describe what the State is doing to increase the number or variety of outlets. The *Timor-Leste* report quoted previously goes on to say: 'On the other hand, these early stages of building a new and vibrant independent mass media have afforded opportunities for a range of measures to be adopted...'[87] But the report does not say how those opportunities have been seized by concrete action. And in *Viet Nam*, lack of money is given as a reason for poor dissemination of information:

> Because of budget limitations, children in mountainous and remote areas still lack an adequate supply of books and newspapers, and may not be reached by television or radio transmission. Since Viet Nam adopted an 'open-door policy,' more and more harmful books, videos, tapes, films, toys and so forth have appeared in the country; however, these are not scrupulously checked and dealt with. Therefore, there is a danger of children being exposed to indecent lifestyles and violence, leading to criminal activity.[88]

But there is no information about what Viet Nam is doing to address these problems. By contrast, India cites similar financial problems, but still it has taken innovative measures to disseminate important information:

> In a country like India, where the reach of the mass media is limited by poverty, inaccessibility and low literacy levels, other means of communication through word of mouth, community events and performances of mobile, cultural troops play a crucial role in providing information and opinion-building.[89]

Some States give excellent information on what they are doing to increase the availability and the ease of utilization of mass media sources. For instance, *Mongolia* reported on its steps to build up the infrastructure in order to give rural dweller access to mass media.[90] And *Ecuador* gave an extraordinarily rich description of what it has done to promote access to the Internet, including requiring

---

[86] 'Ease of utilization' is refers to accessibility, and strictly speaking, it is outside of Article 17. However, the reports should take a holistic approach: States must increase access, accessibility, and attainment of mass media communications if the Convention's purpose it to be achieved—promoting each child's survival and healthy development to the maximum possible (Article 6).

[87] CRC/C/TLS/1, p. 23.

[88] CRC/C/65/Add.20, p. 29.

[89] CRC/C/93/Add.5, p. 100.

[90] CRC/C/MNG/3–4, p. 30, paras. 114–122.

private Internet cafés to allow people with low incomes to use their services without charge (although the reporting was done incorrectly under the Article 13).[91]

The second sentence in Article 17 moves from the duty to ensure diversity in sources to a series of duties framed in terms of the State 'encouraging' other actors. Most of these duties pertain to making the content beneficial to young people. The reports in the survey will be discussed under the headings of each of these 'encouraging' duties.

(a) *Encourage the mass media to disseminate information and material of social and cultural benefit to the child and in accordance with the spirit of Article 29;*

In *France*, the role of parents is being integrated into domestic media policy; 'France is developing policies which seek the right balance in this area. On the one hand, policies aim to encourage greater freedom for children through wide access to the media and information. On the other hand, they aim to provide a proper framework for children's access to the tools of communication, and to hold the various participants—and parents—duly responsible in relation to the information disseminated via the media.'[92]

(b) *Encourage international co-operation in the production, exchange and dissemination of such information and material from a diversity of cultural, national and international sources;*

The spirit of cooperation, exchange and open dialogue between States also seems to be determined by how well the State is implementing its domestic policy on media and communications, which is influenced by economic, political and legal factors. In other words, States have a priority of promoting nationalistic view among their citizenry before embarking on promoting diverse, international views.

In *Canada*, public funds are expended to build national pride among its citizens and the world: 'The National Film Board (NFB) is a federal cultural agency that produces and distributes films that 'interpret Canada to Canadians and other nations.'[93] The Canadian-centered viewpoint applies to films for domestic and foreign audiences: 'As of April 1998, Canada has signed a total of 44 film and television co-production agreements with 52 states. Canadian children's programming is made available in other countries by a variety of means, in particular

---

[91] CRC/C/ECU/4, p. 40, para. 150.
[92] CRC/C/FRA/4, p. 41.
[93] CRC/C/83/Add.6, p. 22.

Telefilm Canada's International Affairs division and its European office located in Paris.[94] The report is silent about international cooperation to increase the flow of films and other materials into Canada.

In *Ecuador*, 'According to the Law on Radio and Television Broadcasting, stations must contribute to the promotion and development of the cultural values of the Ecuadorian nation and pursue the formation of a civic consciousness oriented to the attainment of national goals. National music and artistic values will be especially fostered.'[95]

In *Italy*, domestic law requires foreigners to teach their children the Italian language, while providing for tolerance in Italian schools of outside cultures.[96]

According to Hammarberg, 'it seems that liberal societies have had difficulties to find means of asserting these good values without falling into the trap of formulating State opinions on ideological and political matters. More authoritarian States do not have that problem, though their rhetoric—even when expressing positive values—are not always taken seriously and therefore have less impact.'[97]

(c) *Encourage the production and dissemination of children's books;* is often combined with

(d) *Encourage the mass media to have particular regard to the linguistic needs of the child who belongs to a minority group or who is indigenous;*

Tajikistan reported: 'A lack of resources has made it impossible to publish all the necessary textbooks in all the languages concerned. The textbooks that are intended to provide in the languages of the national minorities of Tajikistan have not yet been published. Under the agreements concluded with the embassies of the countries in question schools will be provided with textbooks and teaching materials in the national language.'[98]

In *Ghana*, the financial obstacles created by having multiple languages is cited in the school environment, 'The Ministry of Education in collaboration with other agencies such as Bureau of Ghana Languages publishes written materials in 11 local languages for use in schools. The provision of written materials in the 44 local languages has been difficult because of the diversity of languages and financial constraints.'[99] It is not clear as to which written materials this applies—textbooks or otherwise.

---

[94] CRC/C/83/Add.6, p. 25.
[95] CRC/C/ECU/4, p. 47 (Article 36, paragraphs 2 and 3, of Law No. 40 of 6 March 1998).
[96] CRC/C/70/Add.13 p. 57.
[97] T. Hammarberg, *o.c.* (note 54), p. 253.
[98] CRC/C/TJK/2, p. 46.
[99] CRC/C/65/Add.34, p. 35.

(e) *Encourage the development of appropriate guidelines for the protection of the child from information and material injurious to his or her well-being, bearing in mind the provisions of Articles 13 and 18.*

In most, if not all, State Reports reviewed for this commentary, the information under section Article 17 was primarily about domestic legislation to protect children from harmful materials, which is not the point of paragraph (e).

Some examples: In *Ghana*, 'the Constitution, The Children's Act, and The Cinematography Act protect children against morally hazardous information from the mass media.'[100] And in *Trinidad & Tobago*, 'The Children and Young Persons (Harmful Publications) Act, Chap. 11:18 was enacted to prevent the dissemination of certain pictorial publications harmful to children and young persons.'[101]

The Government of *Japan*, as part of its National Youth Development Policy, 'formulated the Guidelines for the Improvement of Environment Surrounding Youth in April 2004 in which the Government summarized the items it must work on and items for which the Government is to request local authorities and industry groups'[102] and has many established boards governing the content of film, television, advertising, the Internet, etc. In *India*, 'The General Broadcasting Code, which is otherwise called the Programme Code, prohibits 1) Criticism of friendly countries 2) Attacks on religions and communities 3) Anything obscene and defamatory, 4) Incitement to violence or anything against the maintenance of law and order, 5) Anything amounting to contempt of court, 6) Aspersions against the integrity of the President and Judiciary, 7) Anything affecting the integrity of the nation, and 8) Criticism by name of any person.'[103]

In *Yemen*, 'In order to ensure the child's access to local, Arab and international sources of information and in compliance with the obligations incumbent on the media under Article 102 of the Rights of the Child Act, which provides that the media apparatus must transmit and disseminate material prepared by the Higher Council for Maternal and Child Welfare, the Ministry of Information stepped up its efforts to promote the rights of the child and provide greater scope for the expression of children's issues and views, as well as its efforts to enlighten children about issues and information of interest to them through the audio-visual and print media.'[104]

---

[100] CRC/C/65/Add.34, p. 35.
[101] CRC/C/83/Add.12, p. 172.
[102] CRC/C/JPN/3, p. 53.
[103] CRC/C/93/Add.5 p. 103.
[104] CRC/C/129/Add.2, p. 32.

In *Kenya*, 'Section 15 of The Children Act provides that a child shall be protected from obscene materials. The Film Censorship Board is responsible for censoring to ensure children do not access obscene materials. However they cannot censor TV programs from international sources delivered through satellite and cable service.[105]

In *Mali*, 'law regulated children's access to information as to protect young people from corruption and moral danger.'[106]

In *New Zealand*, the media works with the police to identify child predators, and those engaged in the manufacture and supply of pornography.[107] Similarly, the *Norwegian* government has developed a national education strategy aimed at partnering with parents, teachers and law enforcement to protect children when using the Internet.[108]

4.3. *Implementation As Seen through the Concluding Observations*

The Committee's Concluding observations to the State Parties are grossly absent of clear recommendations for the implementation of Article 17. Instead, the recommendations contain key themes, which include:

- Measures must be taken to educate adults about the rights of children to express their views.[109]
- Traditions and customs in the country sometimes limit children from freely expressing themselves, and State Parties should rescind declarations and reservations to the CRC reflecting traditional and paternalistic attitudes towards children's participation and self-expression.[110]
- Children should be allowed to develop and lead media initiatives on their rights.[111]
- Children should not only be able to consume information but also to participate in the production and dissemination of media. This requires that the media sources have mechanisms for interacting with children and adolescents.[112]

---

[105] CRC/C/KEN/2, p. 49.
[106] CRC/C/MAL/2 p. 53.
[107] CRC/C/93/Add.4, p. 75.
[108] CRC/C/NOR/4, p. 42.
[109] CRC/C/MEX/CO/3, para. 28.
[110] CRC/C/15Add.31, para. 12.
[111] CRC Report, 43rd session, Sept 2006, Day of General Discussion, Recommendations, para. 36.
[112] CRC/C/50, Annex IX, p. 81.

- Media should not be harmful to the well-being of children.[113]
- Monitoring of all media venues should be a top priority for all State Parties to ensure that children have access without being put into danger.[114]

Article 17 requires States to 'encourage the development' of guidelines for the protection of children from injurious materials. In its recommendations to *Ghana*, the Committee expressed its disappointment that 'no mechanism exists to protect children from being exposed to harmful information, including pornography.'[115] In *France*, the Committee's recommendations include a call for better law enforcement: 'the State party take necessary measures, including legal ones, to protect children from harmful effects of violence and pornography, in particular, in printed, electronic and audiovisual media'[116] But the approach towards *Qatar* is different because it appears to put a major share of the responsibility on parents and the children themselves: 'that the State party consider adopting specific legislation and develop mechanisms, guidelines and programmes for parents and children to protect them from information and material injurious to their well-being such as violence and pornography.'[117] And to *Trinidad and Tobago* it said: 'no adequate efforts exist to protect children from being exposed to harmful information, including violence, especially on television.' In none of these cases does the Committee frame the recommendation to fit the duty in paragraph (e) of Article 17: the State shall encourage other actors—like individual media producers and disseminators, or industry-wide organizations—to develop guidelines.

There is also unevenness in the Concluding Observations. The Committee asked *Timor-Leste* to 'improve children's access to appropriate information from a diversity of sources, especially those aimed at the promotion of the child's social, spiritual and moral well-being and physical and mental health,' which just copies the language of the Article without giving any tangible guidance or support.[118] But it made a specific recommendation to the United Kingdom: 'continue to collaborate with civil society organizations to increase opportunities for children's meaningful participation, including in the media.'[119] It is unclear why the Committee would offer suggestions to one State and not to another.

In addition, the Committee often recommends that the State Party utilize the media to further public education on social, health and educational issues. For

---

[113] CRC/C/GC/7/Rev. 1, para. 35.
[114] Ibid.
[115] CRCC/15/Add.73, p. 3.
[116] CRC/C/15/Add. 240, p. 7.
[117] CRC/C/QAT/CO/2, p. 7.
[118] CRC/C/TLS/CO/1, p. 7.
[119] CRC/C/GBR/CO/4, p. 8.

instance, it asked the *Democratic People's Republic of Korea* to 'carry out public education campaigns about the negative consequences of ill-treatment of children in order to change attitudes to corporal punishment, and promote positive, non-violent forms of discipline in schools and at home as an alternative to such punishment.'[120] It has also make specific recommendations to regulate child-related content and child-participation in media programming, and it has cited the danger of invading children's privacy.[121]

---

[120] CRC/C/15/Add.197, p. 8.
[121] CRC/C/GBR/CO/4, p. 9.

CHAPTER FIVE

CHALLENGES

No one denies that the mass media has an extraordinary effect on society. The exact impacts, and how directly they can be linked to the media, as opposed to other social interactions—such as school studies and interaction with family and friends—is hotly contested. While the discussion within the journalism industry usually centers around how to protect 'the public's right to know' through the objective journalism model (see the Code of Ethics in Appendix B), most of the debate on the influences of all of the forms media take place externally toward the industries. Parents, teachers, politicians, academics, social commentators, and others often cite 'the media' as a key source in (primarily) negative influences surrounding child behavior, ranging from bad eating habits, to acts of violence, disrespect for authority, weakening of moral values, erosion of culture, and discontent with self.

While Article 17 requires States to ensure a diversity of sources of mass communications, other Articles call for child protection, which entails laws and law enforcement measures. In theory, there need not be any conflict between these two objectives, but proposals to advance one goal will sometimes conflict with, or be seen as conflicting with, the other one. In these situations, it is important to remember that Article 17 is not just about diversity in sources. First, the preamble states a fact of life—the mass media perform an 'important function' for children and all of society—and by embracing that fact, the Article sets out a value orientation that should guide the debates over conflicts. And second, the State has a series of obligations to encourage others to provide beneficial materials to children, including the creation of guidelines to protect children from harm. By rigorously fulfilling these encouragement duties, the State should be able to reduce the demand for measures that might end up reducing diversity.

The Internet has redefined the traditional role of the mass media, and continues to do so daily. It allows anyone with technological access and any degree of literacy to disseminate their own information to the masses. And it allows all children with the basic technology to have direct access to all of its content, regardless of its potential for harm, unless laws and filtering technology protect them. But laws and judicial rulings that restrict their access could also prevent an adult's access of the restricted materials, which raises questions about conflict of rights under national constitutions, and under regional and global human rights treaties. This includes the rights of parents to protect their children, and to guide and direct their children's exercise of rights under Article 5 of the CRC.

5.1. *Dangers to Children*

Violations of Privacy

The right to a child's privacy is a universally accepted norm (e.g., Article 16), yet children themselves are often the ones who violate their own privacy and that of their peers. With the advent of social networking sites, cell phones with built-in cameras, and easy access to data transmission technology, children can easily create and instantaneously distribute personal or sexually explicit material of themselves or their friends. This direct delivery of inappropriate images and messages can adversely impact the child's life and that of friends and family.

The proliferation of technology in public spaces also threatens a child's privacy if the images of a child are posted in a public forum. Weather, traffic, mapping and security cameras continuously record the public's movements, and the function of these cameras to protect or inform the general public could potentially threaten the privacy of children and members of their families.

Traditional media industries developed guidelines for protecting the identity of a child when part of a media story, although the measures are sometimes inadequate, such as when the photo of child's face has only a thin line placed across the eyes, or the face is blurred while the parents are identified in the caption. However, Internet media distribution sites such as Facebook, YouTube, and other social networking sites allow direct distribution of content without any privacy warnings, and can pose a threat to the child's privacy.[122]

After the death of Diana, Princess of Wales in 1997, the Council of Europe's Parliamentary Assembly adopted a resolution that contained revised protection of personal privacy, including that of public figures.[123] Furthermore, the Assembly called upon States to pass legislation (if none existed) requiring the mass media to adhere to personal privacy standards, or face economic penalties, and for each media outlet to create a complaints mechanism for individuals who feel their privacy has been invaded.[124]

---

[122] International human rights law allows the media to be excluded from court proceedings in juvenile delinquency cases, and for restrictions on reporting; e.g., Article 40(2)(b)(vii) of the CRC, and Article 14(1) of the CCPR.
[123] Resolution on the Protection of Privacy, 1196 (1998) 26 June 1998.
[124] Ibid.

In 2004, the European Court of Human Rights took the same perspective when Princess Caroline of Monaco complained that photos taken of her during her private time by German magazines were an invasion of her privacy. She won the case based on the 'lack of State protection of [the applicant's] private life and her image.'[125] However, the German Constitutional Court also said that the news media had more freedom when reporting on celebrities, since '...celebrities embody certain moral values and lifestyles. Many people based their choice of lifestyle on their example.'[126]

While these cases involved celebrities, they are still instructive. For one, the number of celebrity children and adolescents increases as all of the various medias expand their reach into people's lives, with some of them having 'fifteen minutes of fame,' and others being in the public's eyes for years. More important, every media-and-privacy case involves numerous conflicts of interests and rights. The debates and the judicial resolutions have been adult-centered: adults arguing with adults over the conflicting rights and interests of adults in cases involving adults. Making the world more child-friendly—making sure that young people get 'the special care and assistance' they need, including 'the necessary protection,' as called for in the preamble and in the rights in the CRC—will require adults to change the terms of the debates, and the balancing behind the resolutions, in more and more controversies.

Violence

A 1998 UNESCO global study on media and violence surveyed approximately 5,000 twelve year-old boys and girls from 23 different countries. It concluded that while children are surrounded by both a 'real' and 'media' environment, both contain characters who are rewarded for aggressive behavior.[127]

The exposure that children have to violent images and messages is increasing. In 1970 it was estimated that a child witnessed more than 11,000 total murders on television by age 14,[128] and a follow-up in 1995 found that it had increased to 11,000 *each year.*[129] But perhaps more revealing is the 1996 study that showed

---

[125] Clapham, Andrew, Human Rights Obligations of Non-State Actors, Oxford: Oxford University Press, 2006, p. 397.

[126] Ibid.

[127] UNESCO (Paris). The UNESCO global study on media and violence. A joint project of UNESCO, the World Organization of the Scout Movement, and Ultrecht University (1998).

[128] Bartholow, B.D. Dill, K.E., Anderson, K.B. & Lindsay, J.J. (2003) "The proliferation of media violence and its economic underpinning." In Media violence and children, D.A. Gentile (Ed.) Westport, CT: Praeger.

[129] Signorielli, N. Gerbner, G. & Morgan, M. (1995). "Violence on television: The cultural indicators project." Journal of Broadcasting and Media, 39, 278–283.

57 percent of all television programming contained violent content, and of that violence, 73 percent showed no punishment, 58 percent showed no pain, and 39 percent showed humor associated with violent behavior.[130]

Now, more than twenty-five years later, the Internet allows a child to seek out specific visual scenes and play them over and over, thus increasing the potential of 'acting out' or 'imitating' what they see.

According to sociologist Jo Groebel, 'the impact of violence depends on several conditions: media content, media frequency, culture and actual situation, and the viewer and his or her actual surroundings. Yet, since the media is a mass phenomenon, the probability of a problematic combination of these conditions is high.'[131]

In addition, given the immediate availability that children have to produce video and still images of violent activity through their cell phones, many acts previously undocumented are now 'caught on tape' and distributed among peers. On the other hand, violent images captured on video can also be used in legal proceedings as evidence of a crime.

Violence in News Programming v. Violence in Entertainment

The violent scenes presented in television news programs are considered to be different from the violence displayed in movies, television shows and video games. The journalism industry views the showing of violence as 'obligatory if journalism is to carry out of its core functions of public service by representing the march of human events in all its dimensions. To sanitize reality by minimising or marginalising the presence and intensity of violence would be both hypocritical and paternalistic.'[132]

Groebel attempts to categorize media content into three different modes: (1) Purely investigative (typically news), (2) Message oriented (e.g. campaigns and advertisements), and (3) Entertainment (e.g. movies and shows).[133] But ongoing research since the 1950s contends that violence, regardless of its source, contributes to a violent society. The viewing habits and social behaviors of children was studied in 1986, and then again in 2005. The researchers found that '[The] children's exposure to media violence between ages 6 and 9 correlated

---

[130] National Television Violence Study. (1996) National television violence study: Scientific papers, 1994–1995. Studio City, CA: Mediascope.

[131] Groebel, J. 'Media Violence in Cross-Cultural Perspective' in Singe, Dorothy G. and Singer Jerome L. (Eds.) *Handbook of Children and the Media* (Thousand Oaks, CA: Sage Publishers, 2001) p. 260.

[132] Plaisance, Patrick Lee, 'Violence,' in: Wilkins, Lee and Christians, Clifford G. (Eds.), The Handbook of Mass Media Ethics, (New York: Routledge, 2009), pp. 162–174.

[133] Groebel, J., *o.c.* (note 132), p. 258.

significantly with a composite of 11 different kinds of measures of their aggression taken 15 years later when they were 21 to 24 years old.... [T]hese results certainly add credence to the conclusion that childhood exposure to violence in the media has long lasting effects on behavior through a high-level process of imitation in which cognitions that control aggressive behavior are acquired.'[134]

Sexually Explicit or Provocative Materials

Children are exploited by adults in the creation and distribution of 'child pornography' in traditional media vehicles. The availability of technology makes it even easier for an adult or another child to exploit a child for these purposes. Children are also savvy about technology, and can easily obtain provocative or inappropriate materials from adult-content sites.[135]

False Information

Article 17 does not call for the media to provide reliable, fact-checked information. Disguising fiction as fact can be extremely dangerous if children act upon it. Promoting guidelines for each media industry that calls for disclosing sources of 'facts,' and for requiring 'facts' to be verified, would provide help ensure that children are being provided information they can use to form opinions and make informed, responsible choices.

Mass distribution of information has historically been limited to institutions that have been granted authority to transmit data by the government or those that have invested private resources to build dissemination systems, and often a combination of both. Large amounts of data is collected, processed and made available to a mass audience. When mass distribution of information began, accuracy and fairness was critical to the acceptance by the masses, and to ensure this, a series of standards and practices within various media industries was established.

Article 17 requires the State to make sure that young people have a diversity of mass media sources to choose from, and to encourage the development of materials to promote their well-being. But to be beneficial, the materials must be relevant, understandable, and interesting, and this means that the producers and disseminators must take many things into account, chief of which is the age-range of the children and adolescents in their audiences. And likewise,

---

[134] Huesmann, L.R., 'Imitation and the effects of observing media violence on behavior.' In Perspectives on imitation: From neuroscience to social science. Vol. 2: Imitation, human development and culture, S. Hurley and N. Chater (Eds.), 2005, pp. 262, 264

[135] A question outside of the scope of this Commentary is whether the notions of exploitation and abuse in Articles 34 and 36 extend to children as viewers of inappropriate sexual and other media materials.

the assessment of harms must also take account of a number of things, especially the ages of the youngsters.

Textbooks As a Source of Propaganda

Children from opposing sides within conflict zones are brought together by the organization Seeds of Peace (SOP) to live and play for three weeks in a neutral zone, outside their own countries. While at camp, heated debates about historical 'facts' play out in peer-to-peer sessions where the children defend their right to hate one another based on aggression displayed toward them on specific dates in history. However, closer examination of these exact dates in history, viewed from opposing vantage point, showed major inaccuracies. The children discovered the textbooks in their respective countries offered opposing versions of 'facts'—facts that were taught by authority with the intention of creating national pride.

> In January 2010, eleven Pakistani SOP alumni from Lahore met with their Indian counterparts to finalize the first draft of a history textbook, which compiles both Indian and Pakistani versions of the Indian independence movement and other major events that happened between 1857 and 1957.
> 'The idea of compiling a history textbook came up when we read each others' history in school. There are glaring differences, distortions and omissions of facts of the independence movement in the versions of both the countries, said Mahak Mansoor, a fourth-year graduate student.
> According to her, the Indian history textbook does not have details of the Muslim League movement and has excluded the role of Jinnah and poet Mohammad Iqbal. Similarly, when Shaili Mazoomdar, a third-year law student from Government Law College, Churchgate, visited Pakistan in 2006, she realized that the facts taught on the partition of Bengal in Pakistani schools was different from what she had learned back home. 'The history taught is distorted and this was what made us embark on this project,' she said.[136]

The idea that textbooks and the teaching of history are politically motivated was brought forcefully into the public arena in 1980 by Frances FitzGerald, in her exhaustive research *'America Revised*,'[137] where she compared American historic milestones through the decades of history textbooks. As the textbooks were revised, so was the history.

---

[136] Priya Ramakrishnan, 'Indo-Pak students script a history of harmony,' *DNA—Daily News and Analysis*, (Mumbia, India, 9 January 2010), p. 5.
[137] Frances FitzGerald, *America Revised*, New York: Little, Brown and Company, 1979.

Information, Education, Entertainment and Advertising

Content can be divided into four overlapping categories in order to examine its function in society: information, education, entertainment, and advertising. These broad categories have many sub-categories, and the people who specialize in the production and dissemination of the materials in these sub-categories develop their own commercial, artistic, and ethical standards. In addition, there are professional associations within each media industry that have operating standards and guidelines that they expect their membership to adhere.[138] For example, newspapers will employ journalists, who see their priority as providing balanced, factual information. There are also many other kinds of newspapers, such as those run by churches, which may see their role as providing information through a religious filter, or run by schools, which may see their role as a training ground for students. Each of these producers/disseminators should have their own rules about how their newspaper operates, its rules regarding balanced, objective information and for respecting children.

The courts also play a role in setting professional standards. For instance, the responsibility of the press not to defame private individuals was decided in the case of *Lingens v. Austria (1986)*,[139] where a man being interviewed on a national television program thought the interviewer had led the viewers to believe he had participated in Nazi war crimes. The complainant sought relief at the European Court of Human Rights citing a violation of Article 10 of the UDHR. The ECHR found for the complainant, ruling that an opinion of an interviewer must be clearly differentiated from a fact, and it is the responsibility of the media outlet to make this distinguishable to the audience.

5.2. *Media Literacy*

As the legal scope of the individual's right of 'freedom of expression' and the group-right of 'access to a diversity of sources' is developed in legal circles, the boundary between 'information' and 'entertainment' may change. The journalist' ethical obligation to produce fair and balanced information does not transfer to other storytellers and other forms of media. In fact, some content, such as 'infomercials,' and 'advertorials'[140] and new kinds of 'documentaries,' have taken the appearance of news but are designed to induce particular behaviors in the audience. Adding to the confusion is the fact that many people view the news media

---

[138] For example, see Appendix B for a Code of Ethics for journalists.
[139] Lingens v. Austria (1986) 8 EHRR 407.
[140] Advertising made to appear as objective news reporting.

has having slanted points of view. All of this makes media literacy vital for helping people to protect themselves from abuses, and to gain the maximum benefits from the mass media.

'Media literacy' provides educational tools to help the consumers of media to critically analyze messages to detect propaganda, censorship, and bias in news and public affairs programming, to spot manipulation in advertising, and to understand how structural features—such as media ownership, or its funding model—affect what is being presented. Media literacy also aims to enable people to be skillful creators and producers of media messages, both to facilitate an understanding as to the strengths and limitations of each medium, as well as to create independent media.

Media literacy is an expanded conceptualization of literacy. By transforming the process of media consumption into an active and critical process, people gain greater awareness of the potential for misrepresentation and manipulation (especially through commercials and public relations techniques), and understand the role of mass media and participatory media in constructing views of reality.[141] Media literacy is a vital component when looking at the role of all actors who create media for children and those who work with children to create their own media.

5.3. *Private Sector Guidelines*

The Role of the Journalist in Society

The journalist holds perhaps the most rigid standards of all media professionals, within a context where international and domestic laws in democracies protect free speech, and extend that freedom to journalists and publishers. Those who document events for the masses should prescribe to professional standards for taking care in gathering and verifying facts, and presenting them fairly and objectively (or dispassionately). But not all journalists adhere to these standards. The news-gathering aspect of the profession is split into different aspects, such as narrating events, feature writing, editorials, sports reporting, and issues-oriented reporting. The Society of Professional Journalists has developed a Code of Ethics for the journalism industry worldwide.[142] Journalists who adhere to the Code of Ethics seek a high standard when telling their stories, and demand that their peers do the same.

---

[141]   More information on Media Literacy can be found at: media-awareness.ca.
[142]   Code of Ethics (see appendix B).

On-going training of journalists and editors is an important part of maintaining high standards.

The handbook, 'The Media and Children's Rights,'[143] describes how a journalist should position a child in a story, and when to obtain consent to interview a child by a parent or guardian. While a child's identity is protected by industry standards, domestic or regional laws supercede the industry's guidelines, such as when a child is convicted of a violent crime or has celebrity status.

News outlets are often important distributors of advertising. It is essential that the newsroom is separated from the advertising division in order to avoid the skewing of the reporting. Some journalists and media watchers see a blurring of the boundaries now that newspapers are losing so much of their advertising revenues to competition from the Internet.

Rating Systems and Other Techniques

One of the most controversial challenges to freedom of expression—both the imparting and the receiving—concerns restricting the availability and the accessibility of images of sexual acts, and other materials that invoke sexual sensations.[144] That some content is 'for adults only' is universally agreed upon, but the specifics are not. Attempts to make certain kinds of production and dissemination illegal have been met with freedom of speech claims under domestic, regional, and international laws.

For instance, the Communications Decency Act of 1996 was the first notable attempt by the U.S. Congress to outlaw obscene and indecent sexual material in cyberspace. Among other things, the CDA said that Internet service-providers are not to be treated as publishers, and therefore not responsible for the content that third parties put on their services.[145] In 1998 *Reno v. ACLU*,[146] the CDA was struck down by the U.S. Supreme Court as too vague, and remarked it could have a 'chilling effect' on free speech. In 1998, the Child Online Protection Act[147] became law in the United States. The purpose of the law was to restrict the ability of minors to gain access through the Internet to materials that the Act defined as harmful. However, in *Ashcroft v. ACLU*,[148] the U.S. Supreme Court ruled the law

---

[143] Jempson, Mike. The Media and Children's Rights: a handbook for media professionals, The MediaWise Trust, United Kingdom, 2005; mediawise.org.uk.

[144] Wyatt, Wendy and Bunton, Kris E., 'Perspectives on Pornography Demand Ethical Critique,' in: Wilkins, Lee and Christians, Clifford G. (Eds.), The Handbook of Mass Media Ethics, (New York: Routledge, 2009), pp. 149–160.

[145] Communications Decency Act of 1996 (CDA) United States.

[146] *Reno v. American Civil Liberties Union*, 521 U.S. 844 (1997).

[147] www.copacommission.org.

[148] *Ashcroft v. American Civil Liberties Union*, 535 U.S. 564 (2002).

was unconstitutional. It said the restrictions on children caused restrictions on adults, and this denied the adults' their rights to receive communications under the Constitution.

Similarly in South Korea, where a publisher printed a sexually explicit cartoon in violation of business registration. First the High Court made a distinction between obscene material, which is not protected by the right to free expression, and indecent material, which is protected. Then it pitted adults against children, and ruled:

> But the protection of minors from indecent expression, though a legitimate goal, should not violate adults' right to know. There is a definite need to regulate 'decadent pornography and excessive violent and brutal expression' to protect minors' healthy minds and sentiments. But laws passed for the protection of minors must not prevent adults from accessing constitutionally protected non-obscene material, simply for the purpose of preventing exposure to children.[149]

In Africa, many obscenity laws have been inherited from the colonial past, and raise intriguing questions as to their compatibility with present day constitutions, as well as regional and global human rights treaties.[150] An example from Malawi, *The Censorship and Control of Entertainments Act* regulates the publication and import of newspapers, magazines, books, films and records. Thousands of publications have been banned under this law.[151] Section 177 of the *Zambian Penal Code* prohibits a variety of obscene publications, along with any other material tending to corrupt morals.[152] The *Lesotho Proclamation 9 of 1912*, simply prohibits indecent or obscene publications.[153] These prohibitive domestic laws apply to both children and adults, and have yet to be tested in domestic courts.

It is universally accepted that provisions to protect children from obtaining pornographic or obscene material are needed to prevent the child from harm, and that content should be under parental control. In addition, strict laws can protect children in other ways. For example, making it a crime to use children in sexually explicit productions not only protects those children, but can protect other children who might otherwise be abused by adults (and other youngsters) who consume such materials.[154]

---

[149] South Korea: Constitutional Court of Korea 10-1 KCCR 327, 95 HUN-KA 16 (1998).

[150] Obscenity Laws and Freedom of Expression, Media Law and Practice in Southern Africa, No. 12, January 2000, p. 9.

[151] Carver, R., "Malawi" Who Rules the Airwaves?: Broadcasting in Africa (ARTICLE 19 and Index on Censorship: London, 1995), p. 44.

[152] Penal Code Act, Chapter 57, Laws of Zambia.

[153] Committee of Experts on the Application of Conventions and Recommendations (CEACR), *Worst Forms of Child Labour Convention, 1999 (No. 182); Lesotho (ratification: 2001).*

[154] Obscenity Laws and Freedom of Expression, Media Law and Practice in Southern Africa, No. 12, January 2000, p. 17.

The Association of Sites Advocating Child Protection (ASACP) surveys adult-content sites for terms that might indicate child pornography, and it does this for twenty languages. When offenses are detected, the websites are reported to law enforcement authorities. ASACP also has a Restricted to Adults label as a way for parents to protect their children from viewing age-restricted content. In 2010, ASACP expanded internationally, and introduced the '18–18 Initiative' which requires members to restrict their content to those 18 and older, unless the member's country requires an older age. Another method of control is to require a password for access.

Similarly, the film industries in different countries have adopted ratings to guide parents as to the type of content shown in the film, and many television networks have adopted ratings. As a further measure, many countries have imposed time slot restrictions on when 'mature' content can and cannot be shown on public broadcasting. These are excellent examples of industry-created guidelines that do not entail State-imposed censorship.

However, Article 17 is not about State-imposed restriction of content, but instead requires the State to encourage other actors—such as the various media industries themselves—to develop guidelines for the protection of the child from information and material injurious to his or her well-being. While it is useful to include state laws for protecting children when monitoring or working for implementation of Article 17, since this maintains a holistic perspective to the mass media, it needs to be done so as not to cause confusion about the meaning of the Article. State censorship is not an Article 17 matter.

5.4. *The Role of Libraries in Society*

Public libraries rely on their librarians to determine what books are suitable for children in their communities. The International Federation of Library Associations (IFLA) adheres to core principles, including the Right to Access Information as stated in the UDHR, Article 19. The IFLA believes 'that people, communities and organizations need universal and equitable access to information, ideas and works of imagination for their social, educational, cultural, democratic and economic well-being.'[155]

Marian Koren developed that perspective in her book, 'Tell Me! The right of the child to information,' arguing that the right to information is fundamental in the development of a child. At a Japanese conference on libraries and the CRC, it was said that 'the right to use the library was considered one of the rights derived

---

[155] International Federation of Library Associations, Core Value #2 (ifla.org).

from Articles 12, 13 and 17 and related to Articles 26, 28 and 42,' and added that 'the protective measure in Article 17(c) is not so much about removing bad entries from the library, but the obligation of adults to create a good cultural climate, with good books, good libraries and good librarians.'[156]

UNESCO developed guidelines for public libraries called the UNESCO Public Library Manifesto, adopted in 1994. 'The Public Library is the local centre of information, making all kinds of knowledge and information readily available to its users. The services of the public library are provided on the basis of equality of access for all, regardless of age, race, sex, religion, nationality, language or social status. Specific services and materials must be provided for those who cannot, for whatever reason, use the regular services and materials, for example linguistic minorities, people with disabilities or people in hospital or prison.'[157]

The Manifesto expresses the same idea that underlies Article 17: books, magazines, recordings and other mass media products are vital to children, and their dissemination to all children must be assured.

5.5. *The Participation of Children*

Article 13 of the CRC gives children the right to hold their own opinions (which is an absolute right), and a right of free expression: to 'seek, receive and impart information and ideas of all kinds, regardless of frontiers, either orally, in writing or print, in the form of art, or through any other media of the child's choice' (which is subject to reasonable restrictions). Article 17 is a 'group right' that puts three main duties on the State.

But how does a child participate in the mass media, especially when the child is often considered incompetent by the traditional press? Youth voices are rarely heard in mainstream media stories, while community and scholastic media have emerged to offer children a means for expression within their communities.

Professional media organizations do not offer unedited children's views, though independent child-focused organizations offer training in storytelling and composition, and they allow children great latitude in expressing their thoughts and opinions.

---

[156] Koren, Marian, *Tell Me!: the right of the child to information*, (The Netherlands: Den Haag: NBLC Uitgeverij, 1996), p. 470.

[157] UNESCO Public Library Manifesto, (unesco.org/webworld/libraries/manifestos/index_manifestos.html).

The World Association of Newspapers (WAN) funded the study *Youth Media DNA*[158] to examine how children and youth consume media and where the trends are leading. The study actually drives the media further from child participation. It asks questions about how and where children obtain their news, rather than what the industry could do to make existing news stories more relevant to children, or what they can do to encourage more interaction between children and the producers and disseminators of news.[159]

On the positive side, there are more than 2,000 independent child and youth media organizations[160] outside of schools, and more being created. For the most part, these child-focused media organizations are designed to fulfill a specific purpose, such as skills development or organizational activity updates. However, the unfiltered Internet allows children to have unlimited voice to the world, and they will unless a caring adult intervenes to guide, protect, and instruct.

Legal Aspect of Children's Freedom of Expression in School Journalism

The content in school-based newspapers in primary and secondary schools is overseen by the school administration. The individual student's right to free expression, as guaranteed by the CRC, other human rights treaties, and national laws and constitutions, is not absolute, and a number of factors come into play when children use school facilities and school time to work on school newspapers, and when their materials can affect the interests and rights of others. At these levels of education, the school authorities justify having school newspapers as an educational activity, and this entails the responsibilities and rights necessary for them to ensure that the activities are educational and to the benefit of all.

The Student Press Law Center (SPLC) defends the student journalists' right to a free press and to free speech in the United States. Yet, as the SPLC points out, not all students are protected by the same laws. There is a difference between private and public schools when it comes to rights to a free press and freedom of speech.[161] For instance, according to *Press Freedoms in Practice: A Manual for Student Press Advisers Responding to Censorship*, censorship by government officials, which include public school employees, is not permitted under the First Amendment of the U.S. Constitution. However, the same censorship is permitted

---

[158] Youth Media DNA—Decoding Youth as News and Information Consumers study, World Association of Newspapers, 2007.

[159] Ibid.

[160] Source: Youth OUTLOUD!, the largest independent distribution source of child and youth media stories in the world, New York 2010, with more than 3,000 professional and child/youth affiliates.

[161] Press Freedoms in Practice: A Manual for Student Press Advisers Responding to Censorship, pages 9–11, (splc.org/pdf/adviserspfip.pdf, Newspaper Association of America Foundation).

by private school employees—who are private citizens.[162] In the eyes of the law, the high school principals are viewed as publishers,[163] so they exercise the same prerogatives as other newspaper publishers to determine content. This unnecessarily constrains what a student journalist is allowed to say in a school newspaper.

Arguments about where to draw the lines, and who decides and upon what factors, will always exist. But the lines can change as society changes in its values and perspectives, including increased respect for the human rights of children.

5.6. *The Internet's Influence on the Future*

The Internet is a superhighway of the ebb and flow of information. A free and open connection allows anyone with a computer, Internet access and literacy skills to receive and impart information on any topic, any time. *Information on any topic. Anytime. Anywhere.*

For some, this is total freedom, for others it represents a world turned upside down. Information is a commodity. It is bought and sold. It can provide some individuals freedom and imprison others. But of most concern is that all types of media categories are available via the Internet, and there is no obvious distinction between information, education, advertising and entertainment.

Teachers have expertise in a specific topic and are paid to enlighten others. Doctors have information on healing illness, and are paid to heal the sick. Journalists were once the 'eyes and ears' of the public and paid to attend meetings and events and share their experience with their audience. Political representatives are elected to represent a body of people on governmental issues.

Yet, each of these professions—and many others—are finding their role in society challenged by the free flow of information available on the Internet—and they are fighting for new footing, and, in some cases for their survival. The Media Action Project (MAP)[164] has listed more than 30 legal reforms proposed in the United States for 2010, that in some way or another limit the distribution of ideas to the masses—for a variety of reasons, albeit public safety, child protection, morality, etc.

Consider how much information is available at the click of a button that once required another person to gather it, review it and disseminate it? An investor no longer needs to buy securities through a professional broker, a student no longer

---

[162] Ibid., p. 9.

[163] US Supreme Court, *Hazelwood v Kuhlmeier*, 1988, 484 U.S. 260.

[164] The Media Action Project provides pro-bono legal services for the communications industry with the goal of maintaining a free and open press. (mediaactionproject.org).

needs to enroll in classes to learn another language, a trip to the doctor's office isn't required to remedy an illness, etc.

However, the information age arrived within the home to a population with a varying degree of media literacy. For societies without an educated population able to decipher fact from fiction, large groups can be convinced to take action that could harm society.

The journalism profession—as it has been traditionally known—is in danger of becoming obsolete. While mainstream media such as the daily newspaper and nightly news broadcasts are losing audience, the flow of information is at an all-time high. Data between individuals and mass distribution of information is available to anyone with an Internet connection, yet there is no verification of this information, rumor is treated as fact and visual images can be modified to convince the viewer that what they see is real.

Newspapers have been shifting readers to their online news sites, and the industry has responded by producing shorter stories to attract readers and viewers. While the expense of employing seasoned journalists is high, the costs are not being offset by advertising dollars and subscriptions as it once was. The public feels entitled to lighting-fast information, yet sees no reason to pay for it.

The journalism industry must remember it is an industry because of the Code of Ethics to which it adheres. The core value of the journalist is the pursuit of the truth through fair and objective investigation and reporting. Journalism is the balanced truth contained in a story—through audio, still image, video or the written word.

Unfortunately, the journalism industry created a business model that required many different types of stories to attract larger audiences to increase revenues through the sale of advertising. Most stories in a newspaper or on television do not require the skills and ethics of a journalist. In fact, many stories would attract more readers by containing the views of those readers.

The journalist was originally the person who went places the reader could not access—they'd go and return with the most accurate account of what happened possible. They described the impact of war, they went to city council meetings, they visited far-away lands and talked to foreign people. Their stories took each reader to places the public would never go.

Journalism and Internet chatter must co-exist—and there is an essential place for them both. Democracy depends on it.

As long as *any story, anytime, anywhere* is available online, the public's media literacy filter will continue to clog. The truth has become indistinguishable from the hype and the response is to not trust what is read, or close oneself to only that which is familiar. Day-by-day the lines between information, education, advertising and entertainment continue to dissolve, and the primary contributing factor is the Internet.

The mass media must do better. In the United States the press stands alone as the sole commercial industry that is protected in its Constitution's Bill of Rights. This right requires responsibility, as all rights do.

As an industry, the mass media owes the public the truth, and it owes unbridled access to a variety of sources so each person can determine their own truth. It owes fairness. It owes the public thorough research and balanced reporting. It must place this protected right above their business model and find a way to maintain a place of respect and honor in society. Journalists must go where the public cannot go and find information that individuals cannot, and they must hold public officials and institutions accountable. It is citizens' right to have the truth.

The media business model has marred the role of the journalist. Social networking and citizen journalism is protected as freedom of speech, an individual right—freedom of the press is a collective right.

'In fall 1984, at the first Hackers' Conference, author and visionary Stewart Brand said in one discussion session: 'On the one hand information wants to be expensive, because it's so valuable. The right information in the right place just changes your life. On the other hand, information wants to be free, because the cost of getting it out is getting lower and lower all the time. So you have these two fighting against each other.'[165]

This attitude is a growing threat to democracy. The most deceptive aspect of this phenomenon is that the free flow of information looks and acts like the ultimate democracy. But it is not. The sources of this flow of information must be scrutinized and clearly understood, the originator (source) of the content must be disclosed.

Redefining Mass Media Distribution

The prolific growth of electronic data distribution has caught the imaginations of the business minds, and there is a race to become the primary source of data delivery to the individual. While individuals universally are granted the right to free expression, the mass media's dissemination of those ideas to the public is nearly always for profit in the private sectors, and even State-owned media can take commercial factors in account.

A new distribution source has emerged as a restrictor of data—the information platform. Technology is morphing individuals into conduits of data tapping into

---

[165] "Whole Earth Review", May 1985, p. 49.

the mass pipeline of messages, and the messages are transmitted on technology platforms that require proprietary hardware and software to complete the communication. In an example, the battleground between PC-based technology and Apple-based technology has intensified, with each side becoming more and more sophisticated, and thus, more restrictive to the free flow of information—and there are more systems and various technologies customized to integrate with the system that bids the highest price.

Once someone buys a particular platform (such as an iPod or iPad), and begins to stock it with its personal inventory of data (apps), the decision to change to a different platform later becomes a major financial decision—it would require a substantial investment just to re-purchase the same inventory as previously owned on the former platform.

Technology dependency has not yet run through generations of life, but it is easy to see how a technology dependent society is emerging as platform-dependent in the way information is created, shared and stored. Books, for example, were once exclusively published and placed on a shelf. Years later, the dust would be blown off and the same book could be read by another family member. However, instant downloads of content such as books, music and videos are not as versatile, and certainly not permanent. A change in platform would be the financial equivalent of a fire in a personal library; all books would have to be repurchased to match the new system format.

The handful of companies that control these platforms and the format of content dissemination, can potentially control how all forms of content is delivered to the individual.

5.7. *Revising the Reporting Guidelines*

As mentioned earlier, the Guidelines for reporting ask only one question, and that question is about content: 'States Parties should provide relevant information in respect of: . . . (g) Access to appropriate information (Art. 17).' This has caused serious confusion about the meaning of the Article 17, and the result has been to deprive children of the benefits of a unique and important 'group right.' The only answer to this problem is to revise the Guidelines. And Article 17 is relatively complex; the new Guidelines will also have to be somewhat complex.

The revised Guidelines should request the six types of information that were set out in the section on Implementation as Seen Through the State Reports (section 4.2). Information about: (1) Diversity in ownership; (2) Diversity in the origins of production; (3) State-imposed restrictions on mass media sources; (4) Measures to increase diversity in sources; (5) Statistical descriptions of children's access to the mass media; (6) Measures to increase the availability of, and the ease of use of, mass media sources. The reports also need to say (7) what the State is doing to encourage other actors to produce and disseminate beneficial material, and to create and enforce guidelines to protect children from harmful material, under paragraphs (a) to (e) of Article 17. The revision should also take account the overlapping between the Articles, and the emerging themes of the children's rights movement. This includes reporting on (8) what the State is doing to protect young people from harmful material, beyond encouraging others to create guidelines (e.g., laws, policies, and programs, and engagement with civil society and intergovernmental organizations), and (9) what the State is doing to promote the participation of young people in the mass media, and in teaching media literacy.

Is all of this reporting too great a burden on States, and on the Committee? Certainly the present reporting requirements are at a breaking point for many if not most States, especially in the light of their reporting obligations under all of the other human rights treaties. And the workload of the Committee is already heavy.

With that said, there are two reasons that support a thorough set of guidelines. First, during the twenty years that the Convention has been in effect, the Committee has acquired an extraordinary amount of information on what States are doing to fulfill the other Articles. But for Article 17, there is nothing on diversity of mass media sources, and (with occasional notable exceptions), next to nothing on the 'encouragement' duties. A thorough set of guidelines on the mass media is now necessary to make up for twenty years of neglect.

Second, Article 17 is unique. There is no other human rights provision, and no other human rights forum, that would directly require States to engage with the international community on what they are doing to ensure diversity of mass media sources, and to overcome disparities in access. And yet, this transparency, accountability, and engagement are essential to the modern, interconnected world that is dependant upon the exchange of information. As the MacBride Report urged, every State needs to have a communications policy, and the policy must be developed through both domestic and transnational processes.[166] Generally speaking, States do have communications policies, they are passing media laws and expanding their infrastructures. Economic development, national security, the demands of the public, and pressures from the business community, combine to force them to act. All of this has tremendous impacts on the enjoyment of human rights, for good and for ill.

---

[166] MacBride Report, o.c. (note 6), pp. 203–212, and 254–255, 268–272 (recommendations).

The field of mass media now needs to be fully incorporated into the field of international human rights law and processes. Article 17 of the CRC is the vehicle for doing this. The sheer importance of the mass media in the lives of everyone, and its vast potential for good, and its capacity for harm, justify the Committee in requesting States to give a thorough report on the fulfillment of Article 17, and on related matters such as participation and protection.

CHAPTER SIX

CONCLUSION

Article 17 has been dissected and discussed in this Commentary, which calls for a reexamination of Reporting Guidelines. Given the importance the CRC has granted the mass media, it deserves to be carefully scrutinized by each government when submitting State Reports.

The Value of Original Thought

Creativity is a personal process. Governments do not have ideas. Companies do not think. It is people within those institutions that compose thoughts, and often surrounded by others, the idea comes to life and takes root as a new product, service, policy, etc. Just as 'good' ideas can change the world, so can 'bad' ones. Any type of censorship is meant to restrict 'bad' ideas from multiplying. However, censorship can prevent many 'good' ideas from multiplying—including those that could counter oppressive policies, expose corruption and warn the public about defective products.

That the CRC recognizes the mass media as a vehicle for education is a powerful acknowledgement. At the time of its drafting, the mass media only imparted information, and now it has can both receive and impart information. In those States where citizens are literate and plugged into technology, small ideas can be born in remote areas, and collaboration can ensue from the highest level of thinking within minutes. Online educational programs that have linked classrooms from one part of the world to another have consistently been met with surprising cultural discoveries.

This is the value of Article 17.

All ideas have a source. The source is human, and the source is individual. Awareness is the only requirement for the formulation of an idea. However, for an idea to become mainstream, it must have access to mass distribution. At the time of the drafting of the CRC, the mass media controlled the distribution of ideas. The mass media has many parts that compose the pipeline, and each of them controls part of the distribution process—and all of the parts must generate revenue to support its operations.

All ideas generated via mass media require a collaboration of many other people who control parts of the distribution process. A reporter at a newspaper has an editor, who has a publisher, who has a distribution mechanism that brings the paper to the front door. If any one of the parts break down, the idea is not delivered. And, it is likely that the editor and the reporter, as a collaborative team, make the idea more accessible to more people by making it more relevant to more readers.

Article 17 is the sole legal mechanism addressing the State's duty to ensure the group right of diversity of mass media sources. It is through this diversity that ideas and human rights are strengthened for all people, especially children.

BIBLIOGRAPHY

Books, Articles in Edited Books and Magazines

Abramson, Bruce 'The Invisibility of Children and Adolescents,' in: E. Verhellen (ed.), *Monitoring Children's Rights*, The Hague, Kluwer Law International, 1996.

Ang, Fiona, "Article 38. Children in Armed Conflicts", in: A. Alen, J. Vande Lanotte, E. Verhellen, F. Ang, E. Berghmans and M. Verheyde (Eds.), *A Commentary on the United Nations Convention on the Rights of the Child*, Leiden: Martinus Nijhoff Publishers, 2005.

Archer, David, *Children's Rights: Moral and Legal. Children's Rights and Childhood.* 2nd ed. Rutledge, London: Taylor and Francis Group, 2004.

Atkins, Joseph B., "Journalism as a Mission", in: J. Atkins (Ed.) *The Mission—Journalism, Ethics and the World*, Iowa State University Press, 2002.

Bagdikian, Ben H., The Media Monopoly, Sixth Edition, Beacon Press, 2000.

The Children's Law Centre, *Do You Know Your Rights?*, Belfast, Children's Law Centre & CHALKY Freephone Helpline, no date [circa 2005].

Clapham, Andrew, *Human Rights Obligations of Non-State Actors*, Oxford: Oxford University Press, 2006.

Committee on Economic, Social and Cultural Rights, 'General Comment No. 13: The Right to Education,' UN Doc. HRI/GEN/1/Rev. 8 (2006).

Dennis, Everette E. and Pease, Edward, C, *Children and the Media*, New Brunswick, NJ: Transaction Publishers, 1996.

Detrick, Sharon, *A commentary on the United Nations Convention on the Rights of the Child*, The Hague: Martinus Nijhoff, 1999.

——, *The United Nations Convention on the Rights of the Child, A Guide to the "Travaux Préparatoires"*, Dordrecht: Martinus Nijhoff, 1992.

van Dijk, P. and van Hoof, F., *Theory and Practice of the European Convention on Human Rights*, 3rd Ed., The Hague/London/Boston, Kluwer, 1998.

Echoes, vol. 20, 2001, 'United Nations' Convention on the Rights of the Child (Summary)'.

Eide, A. and Eide, W. Barth, "Article 24. The Right to Health", in: A. Alen, J. Vande Lanotte, E. Verhellen, F. Ang, E. Berghmans and M. Verheyde (Eds.), *A Commentary on the United Nations Convention on the Rights of the Child*, Leiden: Martinus Nijhoff Publishers, 2006.

FitzGerald, Frances, *American Revised*, Boston: Little, Brown and Company, 1980.

Fottrell, Deirdre. *Revisiting Children's Rights 10 Years of the UN Convention on the Rights of the Child*, Brill Academic Publishers, 2000.

Groebel, Jo., 'Media Violence in Cross-Cultural Perspective' in Singe, Dorothy G. and Singer Jerome L. (Eds.) *Handbook of Children and the Media*, Thousand Oaks, CA: Sage Publishers, 2001.

Hallett, Chirstine and Prout, Alan, *Hearing the Voices of Children*, Routledge Falmer, 2003.

Hodgkin, Rachel and Peter Newell, *Implementation Handbook for the Convention on the Rights of the Child*, UNICEF, 2007.

International Commission for the Study of Communication Problems, *Many Voices, One World: Towards a new and more efficient world information and communication order*, London, Kogan Page/New York, Unipub/Paris, UNESCO, circa. 1980, also known as the *MacBride Report*.

Koren, Marian, Tell Me!: the right of the child to information, The Netherlands: Den Haag: NBLC Uitgeverij, 1996.

McPhail, Thomas, J., *Global Communication: Theories, Stakeholders, and Trends*, Third Edition, United Kingdom: John Wiley and Sons, 2010.

Minow, Newton N. and LaMay, Craig L., *Abandoned in the Wasteland—Children, Television and the First Amendment*, New York: Hill and Wang (Farrar, Straus and Giroux), 1995.

Nowak, Manfred, "Article 6. The Right to Life, Survival and Development", in: A. Alen, J. Vande Lanotte, E. Verhellen, F. Ang, E. Berghmans and M. Verheyde (Eds.), *A Commentary on the United Nations Convention on the Rights of the Child*, Leiden: Martinus Nijhoff Publishers, 2005.

Pember, Don R., *Mass Media Law (2003–2004 edition)*, New York: McGraw-Hill, 2003.

Siegel, Paul, *Communication Law in America*, Boston: Allyn & Bacon (Pearson Education), 2002.

Singer, Dorothy G. and Singer, Jerome L., *Handbook of Children and the Media*, Thousand Oaks, CA: Sage Publishers, 2001.

Thorgeirsdóttir, H., "Article 13. The Right to Freedom of Expression", in: A. Alen, J. Vande Lanotte, E. Verhellen, F. Ang, E. Berghmans and M. Verheyde (Eds.), *A Commentary on the United Nations Convention on the Rights of the Child*, Leiden: Martinus Nijhoff Publishers, 2006.

Todres, Jonathan, Wojcik, Mark and Revaz, Cris, *The U.N. Convention On The Rights of the Child: An Analysis Of Treaty Provisions And Implications Of U.S. Ratification*, Ardsley, NY: Transnational Publishers, 2006.

UNICEF, 'Convention on the Rights of the Child,' *YMCA World* (World Alliance of YMCAs), No. 4. Dec., 2001.

Verhellen, Eugeen, *Monitoring Children's Rights*, The Hague: Martinus Nijhoff, 1996.

——, *Convention on the Rights of the Child*, Leuven-Apelsoorn: Garant, 2006.

Wagman, Robert J., *The First Amendment Book*, New York: Pharos Books (Scripps Howard), 1991.

Wilkins, Lee and Christians, Clifford G., *The Handbook of Mass Media Ethics*, New York: Routledge, 2009.

Youth Participation Committee, Canadian Coalition for the Rights of Children, 'Say It Right! The Canadian Youth Edition of the Unconventional United Nations Convention on the Rights of the Child,' Ottawa, Ontario, Canadian Resource Centre on Children and Youth (a program of the Child Welfare League of Canada), [no date].

Journal Articles

Cherney, Isabelle and Nancy Walker Perry. (1996) "Children's Attitudes Toward Their Rights, An International Perspective." Excerpted from "Monitoring Children's Rights" The Hague: Martinus Nijhoff, pp. 241–250.

Hammarberg, Thomas, International Journal of Children's Rights, *Children, the UN Convention and the Media*, Volume 5.

Morrow,Virginia. (1998) "If you were a teacher, it would be harder to talk to you": reflections on qualitative research with children in school. *International Journal of Social Research Methodology: Theory and Practice* 1, 4, 297–313.

——. (1999; reprinted 2003) 'We are people too': Children's perspectives on rights and decision-making in England, *International Journal of Children's Rights*, 7, 149–170.

Shedden, David B. Youth & the Media Bibliography, *Poynter Institute for Media Studies*.

UN Publications and Documents

Abramson, Bruce. 2006. Why is the Right in Article 12 Important? (submission to the CRC Day of General Discussion (August 2006) on a Child's Right to Be Heard.

Department of Conference Services, *A Guide to Writing for the United Nations*, New York, United Nations, 1984, UN Doc. ST/DCS/3.

Hammarberg, Thomas. 1996. "Children, the United Nations Convention and the media", (Background paper for the Day of General Discussion (7 October 1996) on Children and the Media).

Office of the United Nations High Commissioner for Human Rights, *Legislative History of the Convention on the Rights of the Child* (New York/Geneva, United Nations, 2007).

Peeters, Bettina. 1996. 'The Child and the Media,' (Background paper for the Day of General
   Discussion (7 October 1996) on Children and the Media).
UNICEF, *What's Right? Summary of the Convention on the Rights of the Child* (flyer, not dated),
   available at www.unicef.org/magic/briefing/uncorc-html.

Cases

USSupCt, Hazelwood v. Kuhlmeier, 1988, 484 U.S. 260.

Journals

Columbia Journalism Review (2 issues).

Other Documents

Bovoli, Gianluca & Giner, Juan Anotonio, Senor, Juan (Editors), *"Capturing and Captivating
   YOUNG READERS: 50 Editorial Strategies"* Innovation Media Consulting Group, 2006.
Carlsson, Ulla. 2006. Regulation, Awareness, Empowerment: Young People and Harmful Media
   Content in the Digital Age., *The International Clearinghouse on Children, Youth and Media.*
Carver, R., "Malawi" Who Rules the Airwaves?: Broadcasting in Africa, ARTICLE 19 and Index
   on Censorship: London, 1995.
Jempson, Mike. 2005. *The Media and Children's Rights: a handbook for media professionals.* The
   MediaWise Trust.
Rights, Childhood, and Public Agenda: A comparative analysis of Latin American press coverage/
   News Agency for Children's Rights; ANDI Latin America Network. Brasilia: ANDI, 2007.
Youth Media DNA—Decoding Youth as News and Information Consumers study, World Association
   of Newspapers, 2007.
Zermatten, Jean. 2003. *The Best interests of the child from the Literal Analysis to the Philosophical
   Scope,* Working Report Institut International Des Droits de L'Enfant.

Interviews

Cherney, Isabelle. From interview by author, September 2007.
James, Allison. (2007) Research with Children. Lecture given at Institut Universitaire Kurt Bosch,
   and subsequent interview by author, February 2007.

APPENDIX A

CONCEPTS AND DEFINITIONS

Advertising—to announce or praise (a product, service, etc.) in some public medium of communication in order to induce people to buy or use it; to give information to the public about; announce publicly in a newspaper, on radio or television, etc.; to call attention to, in a boastful or ostentatious manner.[167]

Child—Article 1 o f the CRC creates a legal fiction that expands the word 'child' from its ordinary meaning so as to include every human being below the age of 18 years, unless the laws of a particular country set the legal age for adulthood younger.[168]

Communications Model—the basic communications model requires a sender, receiver and a mechanism for delivery of a message. 'It was Harold Lasswell who first precisely delineated the various elements, which constitute a "communication fact". According to him, one cannot suitably describe a "communication action" without answering the following questions: who said what, by what channel to whom and with what effect?'[169]

Media—the means of communication, such as radio and television, newspapers, and magazines, that reach or influence people widely. Media, like data, is the plural form of a word borrowed directly from Latin. The singular, medium, early developed the meaning *'an intervening agency, means, or instrument'* and was first applied to newspapers two centuries ago. In the 1920s media began to appear as a singular collective noun, sometimes with the plural medias. This singular use is now common in the fields of mass communication and advertising, but it is not frequently found outside them.[170]

'Media' can be further divided into types of ownership or control, thus describing the entity that has responsibility for the message content and the dissemination of that message.

---

[167] Dictionary.com Unabridged. Random House, Inc.
[168] Article 1 of the CRC.
[169] MacBride Report, p. 285.
[170] Dictionary.com Unabridged. Random House, Inc. http://dictionary.reference.com/browse/ media.

- **Public Media**—media outlets owned or controlled by the State or government.
- **State-Impacted Media**—Media that requires government licensing in order to operate.
- **Adult-Only Media Content**—material created for excusive use of adults and mature audiences.
- **Private Media**—media outlets owned and controlled by a private corporation.
- **Open or New Media**—media available for interactive access to anyone with the necessary tools, such as technology (i.e. the Internet).
- **Children's or Youth Media**—Media created for and/or by children for consumption for children/youth.
- **Traditional Media**—The profession of journalism is defined by adhering to a pre-determined set of ethics and standards of gathering and reporting the news.[171] Each country, region and journalism organization has its own set of ethics[172] and standards that closely adhere to domestic law and company policies. All journalists who are members of the Society of Professional Journalists, a worldwide professional fraternity, believe: *'that public enlightenment is the forerunner of justice and the foundation of democracy. The duty of the journalist is to further those ends by seeking truth and providing a fair and comprehensive account of events and issues. Conscientious journalists from all media and specialties strive to serve the public with thoroughness and honesty. Professional integrity is the cornerstone of a journalist's credibility.'*[173] Furthermore, journalists strive to: *'seek truth and report it, minimize harm, act independently and be accountable.'*[174]
- **New Media (Citizen Journalism)**—content posted on the Internet, often intending to look like a story produced by a journalist.

---

[171] Society of Professional Journalists, Code of Ethics (see Appendix A).
[172] Listing of codes of ethics & standards, ibid.
[173] Ibid.
[174] Ibid.

SOCIETY OF PROFESSIONAL JOURNALISTS' CODE OF ETHICS

The Society of Professional Journalists' Code of Ethics was adopted in September 1996.

Preamble

Members of the Society of Professional Journalists believe that public enlightenment is the forerunner of justice and the foundation of democracy. The duty of the journalist is to further those ends by seeking truth and providing a fair and comprehensive account of events and issues. Conscientious journalists from all media and specialties strive to serve the public with thoroughness and honesty. Professional integrity is the cornerstone of a journalist's credibility. Members of the Society share a dedication to ethical behavior and adopt this code to declare the Society's principles and standards of practice.

Seek Truth and Report It

Journalists should be honest, fair and courageous in gathering, reporting and interpreting information.

Journalists Should:

Test the accuracy of information from all sources and exercise care to avoid inadvertent error. Deliberate distortion is never permissible.

Diligently seek out subjects of news stories to give them the opportunity to respond to allegations of wrongdoing.

Identify sources whenever feasible. The public is entitled to as much information as possible on sources' reliability.

Always question sources' motives before promising anonymity. Clarify conditions attached to any promise made in exchange for information. Keep promises.

Make certain that headlines, news teases and promotional material, photos, video, audio, graphics, sound bites and quotations do not misrepresent. They should not oversimplify or highlight incidents out of context.

Never distort the content of news photos or video. Image enhancement for technical clarity is always permissible. Label montages and photo illustrations.

Avoid misleading re-enactments or staged news events. If re-enactment is necessary to tell a story, label it.

Avoid undercover or other surreptitious methods of gathering information except when traditional open methods will not yield information vital to the public. Use of such methods should be explained as part of the story.

Never plagiarize.

Tell the story of the diversity and magnitude of the human experience boldly, even when it is unpopular to do so.

Examine their own cultural values and avoid imposing those values on others.

Avoid stereotyping by race, gender, age, religion, ethnicity, geography, sexual orientation, disability, physical appearance or social status.

Support the open exchange of views, even views they find repugnant.

Give voice to the voiceless; official and unofficial sources of information can be equally valid.

Distinguish between advocacy and news reporting. Analysis and commentary should be labeled and not misrepresent fact or context.

Distinguish news from advertising and shun hybrids that blur the lines between the two.

Recognize a special obligation to ensure that the public's business is conducted in the open and that government records are open to inspection.

Minimize Harm

Ethical journalists treat sources, subjects and colleagues as human beings deserving of respect.

Journalists Should:

Show compassion for those who may be affected adversely by news coverage. Use special sensitivity when dealing with children and inexperienced sources or subjects.

Be sensitive when seeking or using interviews or photographs of those affected by tragedy or grief.

Recognize that gathering and reporting information may cause harm or discomfort. Pursuit of the news is not a license for arrogance.

Recognize that private people have a greater right to control information about themselves than do public officials and others who seek power, influence or attention. Only an overriding public need can justify intrusion into anyone's privacy.

Show good taste. Avoid pandering to lurid curiosity.

Be cautious about identifying juvenile suspects or victims of sex crimes.

Be judicious about naming criminal suspects before the formal filing of charges.
Balance a criminal suspect's fair trial rights with the public's right to be informed.

Act Independently

Journalists should be free of obligation to any interest other than the public's right to know.

Journalists Should:

Avoid conflicts of interest, real or perceived.

Remain free of associations and activities that may compromise integrity or damage credibility.

Refuse gifts, favors, fees, free travel and special treatment, and shun secondary employment, political involvement, public office and service in community organizations if they compromise journalistic integrity.

Disclose unavoidable conflicts.

Be vigilant and courageous about holding those with power accountable.

Deny favored treatment to advertisers and special interests and resist their pressure to influence news coverage.

Be wary of sources offering information for favors or money; avoid bidding for news.

Be Accountable

Journalists are accountable to their readers, listeners, viewers and each other.

Journalists Should:

Clarify and explain news coverage and invite dialogue with the public over journalistic conduct.

Encourage the public to voice grievances against the news media.

Admit mistakes and correct them promptly.

Expose unethical practices of journalists and the news media.

Abide by the same high standards to which they hold others.

APPENDIX C

THE OSLO CHALLENGE

In November 1999, a three-day workshop with young people, media practitioners and UNICEF staff which led to the production of The Oslo Challenge, on the 10th Anniversary of the UN Convention on the Rights of the Child. The challenge, directed at young people, media practitioners, teachers, and policy-makers, was designed to encourage a positive relationship between young people and the media. It would lead to the development of the European Young People's Media Network and the creation of the MAGIC website.

The Oslo Challenge

Laid down at a meeting organised by the Norwegian government and UNICEF on 20 November, 1999.

The Oslo Challenge is a call to action. It goes out to everyone engaged in exploring, developing, monitoring and participating in the complex relationship between children and the media. This includes governments, organizations and individuals working for children, media professionals at all levels and in all media, the private sector including media owners, children and young people, parents, teachers and researchers.

The Challenge to Governments Is:
- to recognize children as an investment rather than a cost, and as potential rather than a burden, and to strive to integrate this reality into policy, including that related to the media;
- to meet national obligations set out under the Convention on the Rights of the Child and to report regularly to the Committee on the Rights of the Child on policies and actions aimed at fulfilling Articles 12, 13 and 17;
- to ensure that resources are provided so that children and young people have access to information;
- to explore ways in which, without compromising professional independence, support can be given to media initiatives aimed at providing greater access to children, serving their needs and promoting their rights;

- to recognize that an independent media is fundamental to the pursuit of democracy and freedom and that censorship and control are inimical to the best interests of both children and adults, and thus to create an effective and secure environment in which the media can work professionally and independently.

The Challenge to Organizations and Individuals Working for Children Is:
- to respect the need for independence of the media as a component of democratic society;
- to work together with media professionals to promote and protect children's rights and to respond to children's needs;
- to provide effective media liaison services to ensure that media have access to reliable sources of information on children's issues;
- to facilitate accurate coverage of child-related issues by developing media liaison policies that discourage misrepresentation in the interests of publicity and fundraising.

The Challenge to Media Professionals at All Levels and in All Media Is:
- to raise awareness in the media professions about the rights of children and how they can be protected and promoted by good professional practices or harmed through inappropriate policies or actions;
- to work ethically and professionally according to sound media practices and to develop and promote media codes of ethics in order to avoid sensationalism, stereotyping (including by gender) or undervaluing of children and their rights;
- to resist commercial pressures that lead to children's issues and the rights of children to freedom of expression, fair coverage and protection from exploitation, including as consumers, being given low priority;
- to work to enhance the relationship between children and the media so that both grow and improve in understanding of the positive and negative power and potential of the relationship.

The Challenge to Children and Young People Is:
- to know and understand their rights as laid down in the Convention on the Rights of the Child, and to find and develop ways to contribute to the fulfilment of these rights, including the rights of access to information and to diverse points of view, and to find ways to promote their own active participation in the media and in media development.

- to learn as much as they can about the media so that they can make informed choices as media consumers and gain maximum benefit from the diversity the media offer;
- to grasp opportunities to participate in production of media output and to provide feedback to media producers, both positive and negative;
- to share their opinions about the media with those who can help to support a positive relationship between children and the media: parents, teachers and other adults and young people.

The Challenge to the Private Sector, Including Media Owners Is:
- to take into account the rights of children to access, participation, media education and protection from harmful content in the development of new media products and technologies;
- to make the best interests of the child a primary consideration in the pursuit of commercial and financial success, so that today's children become adults in a global society in which all people are protected, respected and free.

The Challenge to Parents, Teachers and Researchers is:
- to acknowledge and support the rights of children to have access to media, participate in it and use it as a tool for their advancement;
- to provide a protective and supportive environment in which children can make choices as media consumers that promote their development to their full potential;
- to be as informed as possible about trends and directions in the media and, where possible, to contribute actively to forming such trends and directions through participation in focus groups, feedback mechanisms and by using procedures laid down for comment and complaints on media content.

The Rationale

Once the world was flat; then it was round. Now its shape is defined by bundled networks of cables, the orbits of satellites, the hot points where people meet to communicate, reaching out from desert radio post to suburban billboard to the virtual realm of Cyberspace. Tomorrow's world—the world of our children—will expand even further along the global pathways of communication. It will offer the potential for a brighter global future; at the same time, the myriad opportunities of the media will also bring more complexity to ensnare the unready.

The powerful and close relationship between children and the media is explicitly mentioned in the Convention on the Rights of the Child, the international instrument that almost every country in the world has adopted as its promise to children. Article 17 of the Convention "recognises the important function performed by the mass media" and calls upon States Parties to "ensure that every child has access to information and material from a diversity of national and international sources". The same article also encourages the media "to disseminate information and material of social and cultural benefit to the child" and calls on governments to encourage the development of guidelines to protect children from harmful content.

A number of other articles in the Convention also engage the media in the promotion and protection of children's rights. Article 12 aims to "assure to the child who is capable of forming his or her own views the rights to express those views freely in all matters affecting the child". Article 13 also underlines the child's right to participate in the media, including the "freedom to seek, receive and impart information and ideas of all kinds, regardless of frontiers, either orally, in writing or in print, in the form of art, or though any other media of the child's choice". At the same time, several articles aim to protect children from abuse and exploitation, including from "information and material injurious to his or her well-being", and Article 3 is an over-arching reminder that "in all actions concerning children, the best interests of the child shall be a primary consideration".

In the implementation of these fundamental rights, the media are in many ways children's best friend: across their wide diversity—television, radio, film, advertising, the Internet, print products, music and more—the media are able to protect, inform, educate, nurture, entertain, encourage and accompany children and young people in a unique way. But the same media also have the power and capacity to exploit, abuse, misinform, exclude and corrupt children, and in so doing deny them the rights the Convention aims to guarantee. With their substantial and growing influence at the very centre of children's lives, the media represent a potent force for both good and evil in the life of a child.

The relationship between the media and children—and between the media and the Convention—is complex, often misrepresented and far from realising its potential for good. In recent years much work has been done to explore different aspects of the relationship. This has ranged from the effects of screen violence on children to the abuse of Cyberspace by those who intend them harm, from the issue of children's right of access to the media, taking into account the tyranny of distance, the marginalisation of poverty and the boundaries of culture and belief, to the realisation that children's role in the media goes beyond the robotic to the unpredictable, the unexpected, the fantastic.

The power and influence of the media and of the commercial motive have provoked fear and at times a desperate call for control and censorship. Children and young people themselves have shown time and again how, if respected, consulted and engaged in the media process, they can help professionals produce better media. And a number of initiatives have grown to explore these topics, and in particular to see how the media can further the rights of children or at least protect them from accidental or deliberate contravention of their rights.

The Process

In 1996, the Committee on the Rights of the Child, the mechanism tasked with monitoring progress in the realisation of children's rights and with advising on implementation of the Convention, held a theme day on children and the media. On the basis of recommendations from participants, the Committee set up a multi-sectoral working group to explore the issues involved in developing a positive relationship between children and the media, and in particular in furthering the implementation of Article 17 of the Convention.

The working group attempted to begin to map some of the initiatives and resources available on the issue, and to bring together individuals and organizations working in this area, including media practitioners and professional associations such as the International Federation of Journalists. In late 1998, the Norwegian Government and UNICEF responded to a request from the group to initiate a process that would not only continue this work but identify examples of good practice, forge co-operative links among the many sectors involved in the issue and produce, where possible, resources that would help other players to develop the work further.

On 18 and 19 November 1999, as part of this response, more than 30 adult and youth participants from the worlds of film, television and radio, government, journalism, child rights advocacy, advertising and academe met in Oslo to share ideas and experiences in an attempt to identify good practice and gaps in the work done so far, explore possibilities and potential for the future, and recommend practical tools and mechanisms for moving ahead. They considered the relationship between children and the media under five broad headings:

- Children's right of access to the media, including new media.
- Children's right to media education and literacy.
- Children's right to participate in the media.
- Children's right to protection from harm in the media and violence on the screen.
- The media's role in protecting and promoting children's rights.

The OSLO CHALLENGE is the next step. It is launched on 20 November 1999, the tenth anniversary of the adoption by the United Nations General Assembly of the Convention on the Rights of the Child, the most ratified instrument in the history of the United Nations. This date was chosen to underline the importance of the Convention as a global platform for action and rallying point for the many groups and individuals who, in responding to the Oslo Challenge, can become part of the search for new to develop the relationship between children and the media.

In ten years the Convention has been a tool that has been widely used to improve understanding and implementation of children's rights. In the next ten years, however, the world will experience globalisation on an unprecedented scale, and the commercial pressures resulting from this will have an enormous impact on both the work of the media and on children and young people as media consumers and participants. The time is right, therefore, to synthesise good practice in the relationship between children and the media, challenge the media further, and send out a global invitation that will energise people from many different groups to join in the task of developing the powerful relationship between children and young people and the media who shape their world.

The Oslo Challenge signals to governments, the media, the private sector, civil society in general and young people in particular that Article 17 of the Convention on the Rights of the Child, far from isolating the child/media relationship, is an entry point into the wide and multifaceted world of children and their rights—to education, freedom of expression, play, identity, health, dignity and self-respect, protection—and that in every aspect of child rights, in every element of the life of a child, the relationship between children and the media plays a role.

The Future

Building on the work undertaken in preparation of the Oslo Challenge, a number of dynamic processes will be initiated. These will include:

- the production of a resource pack containing awareness-raising, training and other materials for operational agencies to become active in exploring and developing the relationship between children and the media;
- documentation for the Committee on the Rights of the Child to develop further understanding of the reporting responsibilities of States Parties relating to Article 17;
- mechanisms to encourage and nurture relationships between young people and the agencies who work for their rights, the media and decision-makers in governments and industry;

- agendas for research and study, consultation and sharing;
- networks of people from many different sectors who are committed to working together to develop the relationship between children and the media and to meet the Oslo Challenge.

This ambitious process will be undertaken in a spirit of agreement that anything is possible in a world where the media industry, voluntary sector, intergovernmental agencies, governments and civil society all want to pull in the same direction to create a better future for children—a future in which their relationship with the media will be pivotal.